Professional Examina

Strategic Level

Paper F3

Financial Strategy

EXAM PRACTICE KIT

PUBLISHING

PUBLISHING

Published by: Kaplan Publishing UK

Unit 2 The Business Centre, Molly Millars Lane, Wokingham, Berkshire RG41 2QZ

British Library Cataloguing in Publication Data

A catalogue record for this book is available from the British Library

ISBN: 978-1-78415-149-2

Printed and bound in Great Britain

CONTENTS

	Page

Section

Quality and accuracy are of the utmost importance to us so if you spot an error in any of our products, please send an email to mykaplanreporting@kaplan.com with full details.

Our Quality Co-ordinator will work with our technical team to verify the error and take action to ensure it is corrected in future editions.

INDEX TO QUESTIONS AND ANSWERS

OBJECTIVE TEST QUESTIONS

EXAM TECHNIQUES

COMPUTER-BASED ASSESSMENT

TEN GOLDEN RULES

1   Make sure you have completed the compulsory 15 minute tutorial before you start exam. This tutorial is available through the CIMA website. You cannot speak to the invigilator once you have started.

2   These exam practice kits give you plenty of exam style questions to practise so make sure you use them to fully prepare.

3   Attempt all questions, there is no negative marking.

4   Double check your answer before you put in the final answer although you can change your response as many times as you like.

5   On multiple choice questions (MCQs), there is only one correct answer.

6   Not all questions will be MCQs – you may have to fill in missing words or figures.

7   Identify the easy questions first and get some points on the board to build up your confidence.

8   Try and allow 15 minutes at the end to check your answers and make any corrections.

9   If you don't know the answer, flag the question and attempt it later. In your final review before the end of the exam try a process of elimination.

10 Work out your answer on the whiteboard provided first if it is easier for you. There is also an on-screen 'scratch pad' on which you can make notes. You are not allowed to take pens, pencils, rulers, pencil cases, phones, paper or notes.

SYLLABUS GUIDANCE, LEARNING OBJECTIVES AND VERBS

A AIMS OF THE SYLLABUS

The aims of the syllabus are

- to provide for the Institute, together with the practical experience requirements, an adequate basis for assuring society that those admitted to membership are competent to act as management accountants for entities, whether in manufacturing, commercial or service organisations, in the public or private sectors of the economy

- to enable the Institute to examine whether prospective members have an adequate knowledge, understanding and mastery of the stated body of knowledge and skills

- to complement the Institute's practical experience and skills development requirements.

B STUDY WEIGHTINGS

A percentage weighting is shown against each topic in the syllabus. This is intended as a guide to the proportion of study time each topic requires.

All component learning outcomes will be tested and one question may cover more than one component learning outcome.

The weightings do not specify the number of marks that will be allocated to topics in the examination.

C LEARNING OUTCOMES

Each topic within the syllabus contains a list of learning outcomes, which should be read in conjunction with the knowledge content for the syllabus. A learning outcome has two main purposes:

1   to define the skill or ability that a well-prepared candidate should be able to exhibit in the examination

2   to demonstrate the approach likely to be taken by examiners in examination questions.

The learning outcomes are part of a hierarchy of learning objectives. The verbs used at the beginning of each learning outcome relate to a specific learning objective, e.g. Evaluate alternative approaches to budgeting.

The verb 'evaluate' indicates a high-level learning objective. As learning objectives are hierarchical, it is expected that at this level students will have knowledge of different budgeting systems and methodologies and be able to apply them.

A list of the learning objectives and the verbs that appear in the syllabus learning outcomes and examinations follows and these will help you to understand the depth and breadth required for a topic and the skill level the topic relates to.

Learning objectives	Verbs used	Definition
1 Knowledge		
What you are expected to know	List	Make a list of
	State	Express, fully or clearly, the details of/facts of
	Define	Give the exact meaning of
2 Comprehension		
What you are expected to understand	Describe	Communicate the key features of
	Distinguish	Highlight the differences between
	Explain	Make clear or intelligible/State the meaning of
	Identify	Recognise, establish or select after consideration
	Illustrate	Use an example to describe or explain something
3 Application		
How you are expected to apply your knowledge	Apply	To put to practical use
	Calculate/compute	To ascertain or reckon mathematically
	Demonstrate	To prove with certainty or to exhibit by practical means
	Prepare	To make or get ready for use
	Reconcile	To make or prove consistent/compatible
	Solve	Find an answer to
	Tabulate	Arrange in a table
4 Analysis		
How you are expected to analyse the detail of what you have learned	Analyse	Examine in detail the structure of
	Categorise	Place into a defined class or division
	Compare and contrast	Show the similarities and/or differences between
	Construct	To build up or compile
	Discuss	To examine in detail by argument
	Interpret	To translate into intelligible or familiar terms
	Produce	To create or bring into existence
5 Evaluation		
How you are expected to use your learning to evaluate, make decisions or recommendations	Advise	To counsel, inform or notify
	Evaluate	To appraise or assess the value of
	Recommend	To advise on a course of action
	Advise	To counsel, inform or notify

D OBJECTIVE TEST

The most common types of Objective Test questions are:

- multiple choice, where you have to choose the correct answer from a list of four possible answers. This could either be numbers or text.
- multiple choice with more choices and answers – for example, choosing two correct answers from a list of eight possible answers. This could either be numbers or text.
- single numeric entry, where you give your numeric answer e.g. profit is $10,000.
- multiple entry, where you give several numeric answers e.g. the charge for electricity is $2000 and the accrual is $200.
- true/false questions, where you state whether a statement is true or false e.g. external auditors report to the directors is FALSE.
- matching pairs of text e.g. the convention 'prudence' would be matched with the statement' inventories revalued at the lower of cost and net realisable value'.
- other types could be matching text with graphs and labelling graphs/diagrams.

In this Exam Practice Kit we have used these types of questions.

Some further guidance from CIMA on number entry questions is as follows:

- For number entry questions, you do not need to include currency symbols or other characters or symbols such as the percentage sign, as these will have been completed for you. You may use the decimal point but must not use any other characters when entering an answer (except numbers) so, for example, $10,500.80 would be input as 10500.80
- When expressing a decimal, for example a probability or correlation coefficient, you should include the leading zero (i.e. you should input 0.5 not .5)
- Negative numbers should be input using the minus sign, for example –1000
- You will receive an error message if you try to enter a character or symbol that is not permitted (for example a '£' or '%' sign)
- A small range of answers will normally be accepted, taking into account sensible rounding

Guidance re CIMA On-Screen calculator:

As part of the computer based assessment software, candidates are now provided with a calculator, although they can also use a physical calculator. This calculator is on-screen and is available for the duration of the assessment. The calculator is accessed by clicking the calculator button in the top left hand corner of the screen at any time during the assessment.

All candidates must complete a 15 minute tutorial before the assessment begins and will have the opportunity to familiarise themselves with the calculator and practise using it.

Candidates may practise using the calculator by downloading and installing the practice exam at http://www.vue.com/athena/. The calculator can be accessed from the fourth sample question (of 12).

Please note that the practice exam and tutorial provided by Pearson VUE at http://www.vue.com/athena/ is not specific to CIMA and includes the full range of question types the Pearson VUE software supports, some of which CIMA does not currently use.

The Objective Tests are ninety minute computer-based assessments comprising 60 compulsory questions, with one or more parts. CIMA is continuously developing the question styles within the system and you are advised to try the online website demo at www.cimaglobal.com, to both gain familiarity with assessment software and examine the latest style of questions being used.

APPROACH TO REVISION

Stage 1: Assess areas of strengths and weaknesses

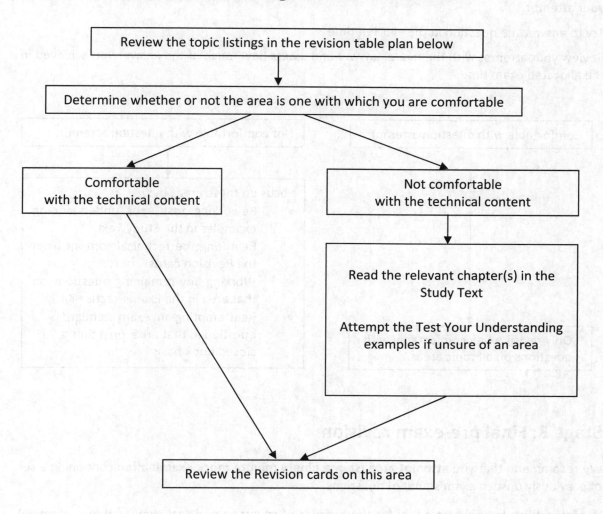

Review the topic listings in the revision table plan below

↓

Determine whether or not the area is one with which you are comfortable

Comfortable
with the technical content

Not comfortable
with the technical content

Read the relevant chapter(s) in the
Study Text

Attempt the Test Your Understanding
examples if unsure of an area

Review the Revision cards on this area

Stage 2: Question practice

Follow the order of revision of topics as recommended in the revision table plan below and attempt the questions in the order suggested.

Try to avoid referring to text books and notes and the model answer until you have completed your attempt.

Try to answer the question in the allotted time.

Review your attempt with the model answer and assess how much of the answer you achieved in the allocated exam time.

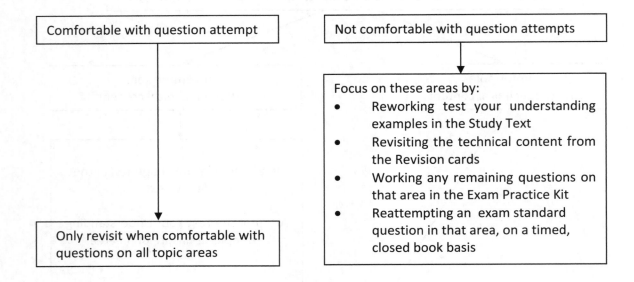

Stage 3: Final pre-exam revision

We recommend that you **attempt at least one ninety minute mock examination** containing a set of previously unseen exam standard questions.

It is important that you get a feel for the breadth of coverage of a real exam without advanced knowledge of the topic areas covered – just as you will expect to see on the real exam day.

Ideally a mock examination offered by your tuition provider should be sat in timed, closed book, real exam conditions.

F3
FINANCIAL STRATEGY

Syllabus overview

F3 focuses on the formulation and implementation of financial strategy to support the overall strategy of the organisation. Using insights gained from F1 and F2, it provides the competencies to evaluate the financing requirements of organisations and the relative merits of alternative sources of finance to meet these requirements. Finally, it develops the competencies required to value investment opportunities including the valuation of corporate entities for mergers, acquisitions and divestments.

Summary of syllabus

Weight	Syllabus topic
25%	A. Formulation of financial strategy
35%	B. Financing and dividend decisions
40%	C. Corporate finance

F3 – A. FORMULATION OF FINANCIAL STRATEGY (25%)

Learning outcomes
On completion of their studies, students should be able to:

Lead	Component	Indicative syllabus content
1 **evaluate strategic financial and non-financial objectives of different types of entities.**	(a) advise on the overall strategic financial and non-financial objectives of different types of entities	• Overall strategic financial objectives (e.g. value for money, maximising shareholder wealth, providing a surplus) of different types of entities (e.g. incorporated, unincorporated, quoted, unquoted, private sector, public sector, for-profit and not-for-profit). • Non-financial objectives (e.g. human, intellectual, natural, and social and relationship). • Financial strategy in the context of international operations.
	(b) evaluate financial objectives of for-profit entities	• Financial objectives (e.g. earnings growth, dividend growth, gearing) and assessment of attainment. • Sensitivity of the attainment of financial objectives to changes in underlying economic (e.g. interest rates, exchange rates, inflation) and business variables (e.g. margins, volumes).
	(c) advise on the use of sustainability and integrated reporting to inform stakeholders of relevant information concerning the interaction of a business with society and the natural environment.	• Limitations of financial statements for incorporated entities, prepared in accordance with International Accounting Standards (IAS), to reflect the value and stewardship of the non-financial capital base. • Principles and scope of reporting social and environmental issues (e.g. Global Reporting Initiative's Sustainability Reporting Framework and International Integrated Reporting Council guidance).
2 **evaluate strategic financial management policy decisions.**	(a) evaluate the interrelationship between investment, financing and dividend decisions for an incorporated entity	• Investment, financing and dividend decisions and the interrelationship between them in meeting the cash needs of the entity. • Sensitivity of forecast financial statements and future cash position to investment, financing and dividend decisions.

Learning outcomes

On completion of their studies, students should be able to:

Lead	Component	Indicative syllabus content
		• Consideration of the interests of shareholders and other stakeholders in investment, financing and dividend decisions (e.g. impact on investor and lender ratios, compliance with debt covenants and attainment of financial objectives). • Determine financing requirements and cash available for payment of dividends based on the overall consideration of the forecast future cash flows arising from investment decisions, business strategy and forecast business and economic variables.
	(b) advise on the development of financial strategy for an entity taking into account taxation and other external influences	• Lenders' assessment of creditworthiness (e.g. business plans, liquidity ratios, cash forecasts, credit rating, quality of management). • Financial strategy in the context of regulatory requirements (e.g. price and service controls exercised by industry regulators). • Consideration of taxation regulations (domestic and international) in setting financial strategy.
	(c) evaluate the impact of the adoption of hedge accounting and disclosure of financial risk on financial statements and stakeholder assessment.	• The accounting treatment of hedge accounting (cash flow, fair value and net investment), IFRS 9 (or IAS 39, before effective date for IFRS 9). • Impact of adoption of hedge accounting on financial statements and on stakeholder assessment. • Disclosure of financial risk, including policies for managing such risk (IFRS 7 *Financial Instruments: Disclosures*).

F3 – B. FINANCING AND DIVIDEND DECISIONS (35%)

Learning outcomes
On completion of their studies, students should be able to:

Lead	Component	Indicative syllabus content
1 **evaluate the financing requirements of an entity and recommend a strategy for meeting those requirements.**	(a) evaluate the impact of changes in capital structure for an incorporated entity on shareholders and other stakeholders	• Capital structure theories (traditional theory, Modigliani and Miller's (MM) theories with and without tax and practical considerations and calculations using MM formulae). • Calculation of cost of equity or weighted average cost of capital (WACC) to reflect a change in capital structure. • Modelling impact of choice of capital structure on financial statements and key performance measures (e.g. ratios of interest to investors and lenders and compliance with debt covenants). • Structuring the debt/equity profile of group companies, including tax implications and thin capitalisation rules
	(b) evaluate and compare alternative methods of raising long-term debt finance	• Criteria for selecting appropriate debt instruments (e.g. bank borrowings, bonds, convertible bonds, commercial paper). • Target debt profile (e.g. interest, currency and maturity profile) to manage interest, currency and refinancing risk. • Use of cross-currency swaps and interest rate swaps to change the currency or interest rate profile of debt. • Tax considerations in the selection of debt instruments. • Procedures for issuing debt securities (private placement and capital market issues, role of advisers and underwriters). • Debt covenants (e.g. interest cover, net debt/EBITDA, debt/debt and equity). • The lease or buy decision (for both operating and finance leases).

Learning outcomes
On completion of their studies, students should be able to:

Lead	Component	Indicative syllabus content
	(c) evaluate and compare alternative methods of raising equity finance.	• Methods of flotation and implications for the management of the entity and for its stakeholders. • Use of rights issues, including choice of discount rate, impact on shareholder wealth and calculation of the theoretical ex-rights price (TERP) and yield-adjusted TERP.
2 evaluate dividend policies for an incorporated entity that meet the needs and expectations of shareholders.	(a) evaluate alternatives to cash dividends and their impact on shareholder wealth and entity performance measures	• Impact of scrip dividends on shareholder value and entity value/financial statements/performance measures. • Impact of share repurchase programmes on shareholder value and entity value/financial statements/performance measures
	(b) recommend appropriate dividend policies, including consideration of shareholder expectations and the cash needs of the entity.	• Implications for shareholder value of alternative dividend policies including MM theory of dividend irrelevancy. • Development of appropriate dividend policy, taking into account the interests of shareholders and the cash needs of the entity.

F3 – C. CORPORATE FINANCE (40%)

Learning outcomes
On completion of their studies, students should be able to:

Lead	Component	Indicative syllabus content
1 evaluate opportunities for acquisition, merger and divestment.	(a) evaluate the financial and strategic implications of proposals for an acquisition, merger or divestment, including taxation implications.	• Recognition of the interests of different stakeholder groups. • Reasons for and against acquisitions, mergers and divestments (e.g. strategic position, synergistic benefits, Big Data opportunities, risks and tax implications). • Taxation implications (group loss relief, differences in taxation rates, withholding tax, double tax treaties). • Process and implications of a management buy-out, including potential conflicts of interest. • Role/function/implications of acquisition by private equity or venture capitalist. • Role and scope of competition authorities in relation to mergers and acquisitions.
2 evaluate the value of entities.	(a) calculate the value of a whole entity (quoted or unquoted), a subsidiary entity or division using a range of methods including taxation	• Asset valuation (e.g. historic cost, replacement cost and realisable value). • Forms of intangible asset (including intellectual property rights, brands etc) and methods of valuation. • Share prices (quoted on stock market or private sale for non-quoted entities). • Earnings valuation (e.g. price/earnings multiples and earnings yield). • Dividend valuation (e.g. dividend growth model, including estimating growth from past or forecast figures and including non-constant growth assumptions). • Discounted free cash flow valuation (including taxation, risk-adjusted discount rate, foreign currency cash flows and sensitivity analysis). • Ideas of diversifiable risk (unsystematic risk) and systematic risk.

Learning outcomes
On completion of their studies, students should be able to:

Lead	Component	Indicative syllabus content
		• Capital asset pricing model (CAPM), including the meaning and derivation of the component, and the ability to gear and un-gear betas. • Calculation of an appropriate cost of capital for use in discounted cash flow analysis (e.g. cost of equity or WACC) by reference to the nature of the transaction (e.g. division or an entire entity), including use of CAPM, dividend valuation model and MM WACC formula. • Efficient market hypothesis and its relevance for the valuation of quoted entities. • Impact of government incentives on entity value (e.g. capital or revenue grants).
	(b) evaluate the validity of the valuation methods used and the results obtained in the context of a given scenario.	• Strengths and weaknesses of each valuation method. • Validity of the results for use in decision making according to the nature of the target entity (e.g. a division, a whole entity, quoted or unquoted).
3 evaluate pricing issues and post-transaction issues.	(a) evaluate alternative pricing structures and bid process including taxation implications	• Forms of consideration and terms for acquisitions (e.g. cash, shares, convertibles and earn-out arrangements), and their impact on shareholders, including taxation impact. • Treatment of target entity debt (settlement, refinancing). • Methods/implications of financing a cash offer and refinancing target entity debt. • Bid negotiation (e.g. managing a hostile bid) including agency issues.
	(b) evaluate post-transaction issues.	• Potential post-transaction value for both acquirer and seller (e.g. taking into account synergistic benefits, forecast performance and market response). • Integration of management/systems and effective realisation of synergistic benefits. • Types of exit strategies and their implications.

FORMULAE AND TABLES

PRESENT VALUE TABLE

Present value of 1.00 unit of currency, that is $(1+r)^{-n}$ where r = interest rate; n = number of periods until payment or receipt.

Periods	Interest rates (r)									
(n)	1%	2%	3%	4%	5%	6%	7%	8%	9%	10%
1	0.990	0.980	0.971	0.962	0.952	0.943	0.935	0.926	0.917	0.909
2	0.980	0.961	0.943	0.925	0.907	0.890	0.873	0.857	0.842	0.826
3	0.971	0.942	0.915	0.889	0.864	0.840	0.816	0.794	0.772	0.751
4	0.961	0.924	0.888	0.855	0.823	0.792	0.763	0.735	0.708	0.683
5	0.951	0.906	0.863	0.822	0.784	0.747	0.713	0.681	0.650	0.621
6	0.942	0.888	0.837	0.790	0.746	0.705	0.666	0.630	0.596	0.564
7	0.933	0.871	0.813	0.760	0.711	0.665	0.623	0.583	0.547	0.513
8	0.923	0.853	0.789	0.731	0.677	0.627	0.582	0.540	0.502	0.467
9	0.914	0.837	0.766	0.703	0.645	0.592	0.544	0.500	0.460	0.424
10	0.905	0.820	0.744	0.676	0.614	0.558	0.508	0.463	0.422	0.386
11	0.896	0.804	0.722	0.650	0.585	0.527	0.475	0.429	0.388	0.350
12	0.887	0.788	0.701	0.625	0.557	0.497	0.444	0.397	0.356	0.319
13	0.879	0.773	0.681	0.601	0.530	0.469	0.415	0.368	0.326	0.290
14	0.870	0.758	0.661	0.577	0.505	0.442	0.388	0.340	0.299	0.263
15	0.861	0.743	0.642	0.555	0.481	0.417	0.362	0.315	0.275	0.239
16	0.853	0.728	0.623	0.534	0.458	0.394	0.339	0.292	0.252	0.218
17	0.844	0.714	0.605	0.513	0.436	0.371	0.317	0.270	0.231	0.198
18	0.836	0.700	0.587	0.494	0.416	0.350	0.296	0.250	0.212	0.180
19	0.828	0.686	0.570	0.475	0.396	0.331	0.277	0.232	0.194	0.164
20	0.820	0.673	0.554	0.456	0.377	0.312	0.258	0.215	0.178	0.149

Periods	Interest rates (r)									
(n)	11%	12%	13%	14%	15%	16%	17%	18%	19%	20%
1	0.901	0.893	0.885	0.877	0.870	0.862	0.855	0.847	0.840	0.833
2	0.812	0.797	0.783	0.769	0.756	0.743	0.731	0.718	0.706	0.694
3	0.731	0.712	0.693	0.675	0.658	0.641	0.624	0.609	0.593	0.579
4	0.659	0.636	0.613	0.592	0.572	0.552	0.534	0.516	0.499	0.482
5	0.593	0.567	0.543	0.519	0.497	0.476	0.456	0.437	0.419	0.402
6	0.535	0.507	0.480	0.456	0.432	0.410	0.390	0.370	0.352	0.335
7	0.482	0.452	0.425	0.400	0.376	0.354	0.333	0.314	0.296	0.279
8	0.434	0.404	0.376	0.351	0.327	0.305	0.285	0.266	0.249	0.233
9	0.391	0.361	0.333	0.308	0.284	0.263	0.243	0.225	0.209	0.194
10	0.352	0.322	0.295	0.270	0.247	0.227	0.208	0.191	0.176	0.162
11	0.317	0.287	0.261	0.237	0.215	0.195	0.178	0.162	0.148	0.135
12	0.286	0.257	0.231	0.208	0.187	0.168	0.152	0.137	0.124	0.112
13	0.258	0.229	0.204	0.182	0.163	0.145	0.130	0.116	0.104	0.093
14	0.232	0.205	0.181	0.160	0.141	0.125	0.111	0.099	0.088	0.078
15	0.209	0.183	0.160	0.140	0.123	0.108	0.095	0.084	0.079	0.065
16	0.188	0.163	0.141	0.123	0.107	0.093	0.081	0.071	0.062	0.054
17	0.170	0.146	0.125	0.108	0.093	0.080	0.069	0.060	0.052	0.045
18	0.153	0.130	0.111	0.095	0.081	0.069	0.059	0.051	0.044	0.038
19	0.138	0.116	0.098	0.083	0.070	0.060	0.051	0.043	0.037	0.031
20	0.124	0.104	0.087	0.073	0.061	0.051	0.043	0.037	0.031	0.026

Please check the CIMA website for the latest version of the maths
tables and formulae sheets in advance of sitting your live assessment.

Cumulative present value of 1.00 unit of currency per annum, Receivable or Payable at the end of each year for n years $\frac{1-(1+r)^{-n}}{r}$

Periods	Interest rates (r)									
(n)	1%	2%	3%	4%	5%	6%	7%	8%	9%	10%
1	0.990	0.980	0.971	0.962	0.952	0.943	0.935	0.926	0.917	0.909
2	1.970	1.942	1.913	1.886	1.859	1.833	1.808	1.783	1.759	1.736
3	2.941	2.884	2.829	2.775	2.723	2.673	2.624	2.577	2.531	2.487
4	3.902	3.808	3.717	3.630	3.546	3.465	3.387	3.312	3.240	3.170
5	4.853	4.713	4.580	4.452	4.329	4.212	4.100	3.993	3.890	3.791
6	5.795	5.601	5.417	5.242	5.076	4.917	4.767	4.623	4.486	4.355
7	6.728	6.472	6.230	6.002	5.786	5.582	5.389	5.206	5.033	4.868
8	7.652	7.325	7.020	6.733	6.463	6.210	5.971	5.747	5.535	5.335
9	8.566	8.162	7.786	7.435	7.108	6.802	6.515	6.247	5.995	5.759
10	9.471	8.983	8.530	8.111	7.722	7.360	7.024	6.710	6.418	6.145
11	10.368	9.787	9.253	8.760	8.306	7.887	7.499	7.139	6.805	6.495
12	11.255	10.575	9.954	9.385	8.863	8.384	7.943	7.536	7.161	6.814
13	12.134	11.348	10.635	9.986	9.394	8.853	8.358	7.904	7.487	7.103
14	13.004	12.106	11.296	10.563	9.899	9.295	8.745	8.244	7.786	7.367
15	13.865	12.849	11.938	11.118	10.380	9.712	9.108	8.559	8.061	7.606
16	14.718	13.578	12.561	11.652	10.838	10.106	9.447	8.851	8.313	7.824
17	15.562	14.292	13.166	12.166	11.274	10.477	9.763	9.122	8.544	8.022
18	16.398	14.992	13.754	12.659	11.690	10.828	10.059	9.372	8.756	8.201
19	17.226	15.679	14.324	13.134	12.085	11.158	10.336	9.604	8.950	8.365
20	18.046	16.351	14.878	13.590	12.462	11.470	10.594	9.818	9.129	8.514

Periods	Interest rates (r)									
(n)	11%	12%	13%	14%	15%	16%	17%	18%	19%	20%
1	0.901	0.893	0.885	0.877	0.870	0.862	0.855	0.847	0.840	0.833
2	1.713	1.690	1.668	1.647	1.626	1.605	1.585	1.566	1.547	1.528
3	2.444	2.402	2.361	2.322	2.283	2.246	2.210	2.174	2.140	2.106
4	3.102	3.037	2.974	2.914	2.855	2.798	2.743	2.690	2.639	2.589
5	3.696	3.605	3.517	3.433	3.352	3.274	3.199	3.127	3.058	2.991
6	4.231	4.111	3.998	3.889	3.784	3.685	3.589	3.498	3.410	3.326
7	4.712	4.564	4.423	4.288	4.160	4.039	3.922	3.812	3.706	3.605
8	5.146	4.968	4.799	4.639	4.487	4.344	4.207	4.078	3.954	3.837
9	5.537	5.328	5.132	4.946	4.772	4.607	4.451	4.303	4.163	4.031
10	5.889	5.650	5.426	5.216	5.019	4.833	4.659	4.494	4.339	4.192
11	6.207	5.938	5.687	5.453	5.234	5.029	4.836	4.656	4.486	4.327
12	6.492	6.194	5.918	5.660	5.421	5.197	4.988	4.793	4.611	4.439
13	6.750	6.424	6.122	5.842	5.583	5.342	5.118	4.910	4.715	4.533
14	6.982	6.628	6.302	6.002	5.724	5.468	5.229	5.008	4.802	4.611
15	7.191	6.811	6.462	6.142	5.847	5.575	5.324	5.092	4.876	4.675
16	7.379	6.974	6.604	6.265	5.954	5.668	5.405	5.162	4.938	4.730
17	7.549	7.120	6.729	6.373	6.047	5.749	5.475	5.222	4.990	4.775
18	7.702	7.250	6.840	6.467	6.128	5.818	5.534	5.273	5.033	4.812
19	7.839	7.366	6.938	6.550	6.198	5.877	5.584	5.316	5.070	4.843
20	7.963	7.469	7.025	6.623	6.259	5.929	5.628	5.353	5.101	4.870

FORMULAE

DVM

$$P_0 = \frac{d_1}{k_e - g}$$

$$k_e = \frac{d_1}{P_0} + g$$

$$g = r \times b$$

CAPM

$$k = R_f + [R_m - R_f]\beta$$

$$\beta_{eu} = \beta_{eg}\left[\frac{V_E}{V_E + V_D[1-t]}\right] + \beta_d\left[\frac{V_D[1-t]}{V_E + V_D[1-t]}\right]$$

$$\beta_{eg} = \beta_{eu} + [\beta_{eu} - \beta_d]\left[\frac{V_D[1-t]}{V_E}\right]$$

WACC

$$WACC = k_{eg}\left[\frac{V_E}{V_E + V_D}\right] + k_d[1-t]\left[\frac{V_D}{V_E + V_D}\right]$$

FX, interest rates & inflation

$$F_0 = S_0 \times \frac{[1 + r\,var]}{[1 + r\,base]}$$

$$S_1 = S_0 \times \frac{[1 + r\,var]}{[1 + r\,base]}$$

$$(1 + r_{nominal}) = (1 + r_{real}) \times (1 + \text{inflation})$$

M&M

$$V_g = V_u + TB$$

$$k_{eg} = k_{eu} + [k_{eu} - k_d]\left[\frac{V_D[1-t]}{V_E}\right]$$

$$WACC = k_{eu}\left[1 - \left[\frac{V_D t}{V_E + V_D}\right]\right]$$

TERP

$$TERP = \frac{1}{N+1}[(N \times \text{cum rights price}) + \text{issue price}]$$

$$\text{Yield-adjusted TERP} = \frac{1}{N+1}[(N \times \text{cum rights price}) + \text{issue price} \times (Y_{new}/Y_{old})]$$

Section 1

OBJECTIVE TEST QUESTIONS

SYLLABUS SECTION A: FORMULATION OF FINANCIAL STRATEGY

1   **Which of the following parties is least likely to benefit from risky strategies that increase risk and expected return for a company?**

    A   Creditors

    B   Chief executive officers

    C   Chief financial officers

    D   Shareholders

2   **TTT is a listed company.**

In its recent annual report, TTT has defined its three financial objectives as follows:

- To increase dividends by 10% a year.
- To keep gearing below 40%.
- To expand by internal growth and/or by horizontal integration via acquisition of companies operating in the same industry sector.

Which of the following is NOT a valid criticism of TTT's financial objectives?

    A   There should be a specific reference made to maximising shareholder wealth

    B   The gearing objective is too vague

    C   The expansion objective should contain numbers so that its achievement can be measured

    D   The dividend growth objective should be linked to company performance

3   **Which TWO of the following are valid differences between the objectives of for-profit and not-for-profit entities?**

    A   For-profit entities primarily aim to maximise shareholder wealth whereas not-for-profit entities don't

    B   Not-for-profit entities aim to satisfy a wide range of stakeholders whereas for-profit entities only aim to satisfy shareholders

    C   Not-for-profit entities don't have financial objectives but for-profit entities do

    D   Not-for-profit entities tend to be most concerned about value for money whereas for-profit entities tend to prioritise shareholder wealth maximisation

4   **Managers of businesses sometimes exploit the agency problem to pursue their own rather than the business's interests.**

In doing so, which of the following pairs of factors are likely to have enabled managers to have run the company in their own interests?

A   Low levels of management accountability and shareholder access to the same information as management

B   High levels of management accountability and management access to better information than the shareholders

C   High levels of management accountability and shareholder access to the same information as management

D   Low levels of management accountability and management access to better information than the shareholders

5   **Cool Co is an entity that was set up by the government of Country C to produce electricity for the country's citizens.**

Five years ago it was privatised as the government of Country C opened up the energy market to competition. The shares of Cool Co are now owned by both private investors and institutions, and are traded on Country C's stock market.

What kind of entity is Cool Co?

A   Private sector, for-profit entity

B   Private sector, not-for-profit entity

C   Public sector, for-profit entity

D   Public sector, not-for-profit entity

6   **Pilchard Co is a listed company which has 1 million $0.25 par value ordinary shares in issue, and $800,000 worth of $100 par value bonds. The shares and the bonds are trading at $1.47 and $94 respectively.**

What is the gearing ratio of Pilchard Co, calculated as [debt/equity] and using market values?

A   51.2%

B   33.8%

C   12.8%

D   11.3%

7   **The share price of Qat Co rose from $6.10 to $6.45 last year. During the year, the company paid out a dividend of $0.30 per share.**

What was the annual return to investors last year?

A   4.9%

B   5.7%

C   10.1%

D   10.7%

8 **Your manager has asked you to compute the Return on Equity for your company.**

Which of the following profit figures would you use in the calculation?

A   Gross profit

B   Net profit

C   Operating profit

D   EBITDA

9 **The P/E ratios of Zoo Co and Ungg Co are 10 and 6 respectively.**

Which TWO of the following statements are definitely correct based on this information?

A   Ungg Co is an unquoted company and Zoo Co is a quoted company

B   Zoo Co's earnings yield is lower than Ungg Co's

C   The market perception of Zoo Co is better than that of Ungg Co

D   The risk associated with Zoo Co must be higher than the risk associated with Ungg Co

E   Ungg Co's share price is lower than Zoo Co's

10 **An investor in Doodson Co has calculated that the company's current dividend yield is 8% and that its dividend payout ratio is 20%**

What is the P/E ratio of Doodson Co?

A   0.4

B   1.6

C   2.5

D   16

11 **Chmura Co has the following accounting ratios, based on its most recent financial statements:**

Operating profit margin = 18%

Interest cover = 2 times

Gross profit margin = 35%

Asset turnover = 1.0

What is the return on capital employed of Chmura Co?

A   17.5%

B   18.0%

C   35.0%

D   It is impossible to tell from such limited information

12   Maximisation of shareholder wealth is MOST likely to be the primary objective of a:

A   Private sector, for-profit entity

B   Private sector, not-for-profit entity

C   Public sector, for-profit entity

D   Public sector, not-for-profit entity

13   Given the following information about a company:

Sales = $1,000

Cost of goods sold = $600

Operating expenses = $200

Interest expenses = $50

Tax rate = 34%

What are the gross and operating profit margins, respectively?

A   20%; 15%

B   40%; 20%

C   40%; 10%

D   20%; 10%

14   Paragon Co's operating profit is $100,000, interest expense is $25,000, and earnings before tax is $75,000.

What is Paragon Co's interest cover ratio?

A   1

A   3

C   4

D   7

15   All else equal, an entity's sensitivity to swings in the business cycle is higher when:

A   variable and fixed costs are roughly in the same proportion

B   the firm has low operating leverage

C   fixed costs are the highest portion of its expenses

D   variable costs are the highest portion of its expenses

16   What is the effect on prices of US imports and exports when the US dollar depreciates?

A   Import prices will increase and export prices will decrease

B   Import prices and export prices will increase

C   Import prices will decrease and export prices will increase

D   Import prices and export prices will decrease

17 **If the exchange rate moves from EUR/USD 0.95 (i.e. EUR 1 = USD 0.95) to EUR/USD 1.10 (i.e. EUR 1 = USD 1.10), then the euro has:**

   A   depreciated and Europeans will find US goods cheaper

   B   appreciated and Europeans will find US goods more expensive

   C   appreciated and Europeans will find US goods cheaper

   D   depreciated and Europeans will find US goods more expensive

18 **Squirm Co generated earnings of $2.2 million in 20X1. It has an objective to achieve a compound annual growth in earnings of 5% per annum.**

   It has just reported an earnings figure of $2.9 million in 20X6.

   What is the company's compound annual growth in earnings?

   A   31.8%

   B   6.4%

   C   5.7%

   D   4.7%

19 **Julie Co has paid the following dividends in recent years:**

	20X4	20X5	20X6	20X7	20X8
Dividend per share	0.20	0.22	0.23	0.25	0.28

   What is the company's compound annual growth in dividends since 20X4?

   A   7.0%

   B   10.0%

   C   8.0%

   D   8.8%

20 **VUE Co has paid the following dividends in recent years:**

	20X4	20X5	20X6	20X7	20X8
Total dividend ($m)	120	130	135	150	170
Number of shares (m)	10	10	10	12	13

   What is the company's compound annual growth in dividend per share since 20X4?

   A   2.2%

   B   6.8%

   C   9.0%

   D   9.1%

21 **Hannah Co is based in country H, where the functional currency is the H$.**

The spot rate for the H$ to the euro (EUR) is H$/EUR 6.250 (that is H$ 1 = EUR 6.250).

The expected interest rates in the eurozone and country H respectively are 2% and 6% over the next year.

What is the forecast forward rate of exchange in one year's time using the interest rate parity theory?

A   H$/EUR 6.014

B   H$/EUR 2.083

C   H$/EUR 6.495

D   H$/EUR 18.750

22 **Jo Co has suppliers and customers in many different countries around the world, so the directors of Jo Co monitor movements in exchange rates closely, using interest rate parity theory to estimate the likely future exchange rates.**

The current exchange rate between the British pound (GBP) and the euro (EUR) is GBP/EUR 1.2400 (that is GBP 1 = EUR 1.2400), and the expected interest rates in the UK and the eurozone respectively are 0.5% and 0.75% over the next year.

What is the forecast forward rate of exchange in one year's time using the interest rate parity theory?

A   GBP/EUR 1.2112

B   GBP/EUR 1.2369

C   GBP/EUR 1.2431

D   GBP/EUR 1.2695

23 **The current exchange rate between the British pound (GBP) and the euro (EUR) is GBP/EUR 1.2075 (that is GBP 1 = EUR 1.2075), and the GBP is expected to appreciate by approximately 2% per year over the next few years.**

What is the expected rate of exchange in two years' time?

A   GBP/EUR 1.2317

B   GBP/EUR 1.2563

C   GBP/EUR 1.1838

D   GBP/EUR 1.1606

24   **W Co is based in country W (functional currency W$) and it makes some purchases from the eurozone, denominated in euros (EUR). Purchases in 1 year's time are expected to be EUR 100,000. The financial director of W Co is attempting to estimate the likely exchange rate in 1 year's time, so that she can assess the likely value of the entity's foreign currency expenditure.**

The spot rate of exchange is W$/EUR 1.9900 (that is W$ 1 = EUR 1.9900). Interest rates in the eurozone and country W are expected to be 1% and 8% respectively over the next year.

What is the expected spot in 1 year's time, using the expectations theory, and what is the expected value of the EUR sales when translated into W$?

	Exchange rate	Value of expenditure
A	W$/EUR 2.1279	W$ 212,792
B	W$/EUR 2.1279	W$ 46,995
C	W$/EUR 1.8610	W$ 186,100
D	W$/EUR 1.8610	W$ 53,735

25   **CC Co is based in country C (functional currency C$) and it makes some sales in the USA, denominated in US dollars (USD).**

The spot rate of exchange is C$/USD 1.1144 (that is C$ 1 = USD 1.1144). Interest rates in the USA and country C are expected to be 3% and 5% respectively over the next few years.

What is the expected rate of exchange in 6 months' time, using the expectations theory?

A   C$/USD 1.1252

B   C$/USD 1.0932

C   C$/USD 1.1037

D   C$/USD 1.1360

26   **Mana Co is about to prepare a sustainability report for the first time, following the Global Reporting Initiative Guidelines. The directors are currently preparing the section covering General Standard Disclosures.**

Which THREE of the following headings should appear in this section?

A   Society

B   Strategy and Analysis

C   Human Rights

D   Stakeholder Engagement

E   Governance

27 **Which THREE of the following are objectives of Integrated Reporting, as identified by the International Integrated Reporting Council (IIRC)?**

  A   To improve the quality of information available to providers of financial capital

  B   To support integrated thinking and decision making

  C   To communicate the impacts of economic, environmental and social and governance performance

  D   To increase the quantity of information available to providers of financial capital

  E   To provide a more cohesive and efficient approach to corporate reporting

28 **Which THREE of the following are defined by the Global Reporting Initiative as being Principles for Defining Report Content?**

  A   Sustainability context

  B   Clarity

  C   Comparability

  D   Materiality

  E   Completeness

29 **If an entity is unable to make all the standard disclosures as required by the Global Reporting Initiative's 'G4' guidelines, which of the following is true?**

  A   The entity is not allowed to state that its sustainability report has been produced in accordance with the guidelines

  B   The entity must state what information has been omitted and why it has been omitted

  C   The entity must state what information has been omitted, but not necessarily why it has been omitted

  D   The entity can still state that the sustainability report has been produced in accordance with the guidelines, without any further disclosure of the information omitted

30 **Mountain Co is a well-established manufacturing company with operations in many countries. Its products have an excellent reputation.**

  In Mountain Co's Integrated Report, how would it present this information?

  A   It would not disclose this information explicitly

  B   As part of its disclosure of social and relationship capitals

  C   As part of its disclosure of intellectual capitals

  D   As part of its disclosure of manufactured capitals

31   Which of the following statements best describes the link between sustainability reporting and integrated reporting?

    A   there is no link between sustainability reporting and integrated reporting

    B   sustainability reporting and integrated reporting are the same

    C   integrated reporting is an integral part of sustainability reporting

    D   sustainability reporting is an integral part of integrated reporting

32   **Loose Co has prepared a draft Integrated Report following the International Integrated Reporting Council's <IR> Framework.**

Which THREE of the headings below have been placed in the wrong section of the report?

Guiding principles

    A   Disclosures on Management Approach (DMA)

    B   Strategic focus and future orientation

    C   Risks and opportunities

    D   Connectivity of information

Content elements

    E   Organisational overview and external environment

    F   Consistency and comparability

    G   Strategy and resource allocation

    H   Performance

33   Which TWO of the following are most likely to increase the wealth of an all-equity financed entity's shareholders?

    A   Paying out a large dividend

    B   Investing in a new project with a positive net present value

    C   Raising new equity finance

    D   Raising new debt finance

34   When financial managers are planning financial strategy for an entity, the impact of regulatory requirements should be considered.

Which of the following is NOT normally an objective of a regulatory body?

    A   The protection of customers

    B   The promotion of competition

    C   The promotion of social objectives

    D   The protection of shareholders

35 **Thursday Co has an AAA credit rating and Cass Co has an A rating.**

Enter the correct word from the choices given:

Thursday Co will probably find it _____(easier/harder) to raise debt finance than Cass Co.

The rate of interest on borrowings is likely to be _____(higher/lower) for Thursday Co than Cass Co.

36 **The managers of Green Co are trying to identify the optimum amount of cash to hold.**

Enter the correct phrase from the choices given:

Holding _____ (too much/too little) cash will potentially leave the entity subject to liquidity problems and possible liquidation.

Holding _____ (too much/too little) cash has an opportunity cost (lost interest on deposits, or returns on attractive investments).

Holding _____ (too much/too little) cash leaves an entity vulnerable to a takeover bid.

37 **Which of the following is NOT a valid reason for a business to hold cash and marketable securities?**

A   to meet future needs

B   to maintain adequate cash needed for transactions

C   to satisfy compensating balance requirements

D   to earn maximum returns on investment assets

38 **Vischer Concrete has $1.2 million in assets that are currently financed with 100% equity finance. Vischer's earnings before interest and tax (EBIT) is $300,000 and its tax rate is 30%.**

If Vischer changes its capital structure to include 40% debt, what is Vischer's return on equity (ROE) before and after the change? (Assume that the interest rate on debt is 5%.)

	ROE at 100% equity	ROE at 60% equity
A	17.5%	37.5%
B	17.5%	26.8%
C	25.0%	26.8%
D	25.0%	37.5%

39   Audre Co has the following financial objectives:

- to achieve an average dividend growth of at least 7% per annum
- to keep its gearing, measured as [debt/(debt + equity)] by market value, below 30%

In the last three years, Audre Co's dividend has grown from $0.55 million to $0.70 million.

Audre Co has 2 million $0.50 shares in issue, trading at $1.24, and 10,000 bonds with a par value of $100 and a market value of $105.

Which of the objectives has Audre Co achieved?

A   Neither objective

B   Just the gearing objective

C   Just the dividend growth objective

D   Both objectives

40   Dunk Co has just reported a profit before interest and tax of $25 million. It has a 6% interest bank loan of $60 million, which carries an interest cover covenant (based on profit before interest and tax) of 4 times.

Dunk Co plans to borrow an additional $40 million, at 5% interest, from another bank to finance a new investment project.

What is the likely interest cover if the new finance is raised, and is the covenant likely to be breached?

	Interest cover	Covenant
A	4.46	Breached
B	4.46	Not breached
C	6.94	Breached
D	6.94	Not breached

41   Thiago Co is a UK based company that makes sales to US customers. It generated revenue of USD 1.50 million last year and its cost of sales was GBP 0.67 million. The exchange rate at the year-end was GBP/USD 1.6500 (that is GBP 1 = USD 1.6500).

In the coming year, selling prices are expected to increase by 4% and sales volumes are expected to stay constant.

If the exchange rate is likely to stay constant, what will Thiago Co's gross profit margin be in the coming year?

A   26.3%

B   29.1%

C   55.3%

D   57.1%

42 **If a company has a fixed rate borrowing but interest rates subsequently fall, the market value of the borrowing would be affected. To hedge this, the company could enter into an interest rate swap, swapping the fixed rate on the borrowing for a floating rate.**

Which of the following describes the correct treatment under hedge accounting rules (IAS 39)?

A The borrowing would be at cost on the statement of financial position and the swap would be at cost on the statement of financial position with any gain or loss going to the statement of profit or loss

B The borrowing would be at fair value on the statement of financial position and the swap would be at fair value on the statement of financial position with any gain or loss being recorded in other comprehensive income

C The borrowing would be at cost on the statement of financial position and the swap would be at fair value on the statement of financial position, with any gain or loss going to the statement of profit or loss

D The borrowing would be at fair value on the statement of financial position with any gain or loss going to the statement of profit or loss, and the swap would be at fair value on the statement of financial position with any gain or loss going to the statement of profit or loss

43 **Beer Co is a US based company whose functional currency is the US dollar (USD).**

It acquired 100% of the issued share capital of Wine Co for GBP 1 million during its financial year ended 31 December 20X1. The purchase was partially financed by a loan for GBP 800,000 and this loan is designated by Beer Co as a hedging instrument.

Which of the following describes the accounting treatment required for gains and losses on the investment and its hedging instrument?

A Gains or losses on the matched investment and the hedging instrument are recorded in other comprehensive income. Gains or losses on the unmatched amount are recognised in the statement of profit or loss each year

B Gains or losses on both the investment and the hedging instrument are all recognised separately in the statement of profit or loss each year

C Gains or losses on the matched investment and the hedging instrument are netted off. Gains or losses on the unmatched amount are recognised in other comprehensive income each year

D Gains or losses on both the investment and the hedging instrument are all recognised separately in other comprehensive income each year

44 Which **THREE** of the following are conditions which must exist in order for hedge accounting to be permitted for a cash flow hedge under IAS 39 Financial Instruments: Recognition and Measurement?

    A   The hedge is expected to be at least 95% effective

    B   There is formal designation and documentation of the hedging relationship at the inception of the hedge

    C   The forecast transaction that is the subject of the hedge must be highly probable and must present an exposure to variations in cash flows that could ultimately affect profit or loss

    D   The effectiveness of the hedge has to be verified by the entity's auditors

    E   The hedge is assessed on an ongoing basis and has actually been highly effective throughout the financial reporting periods for which it was designated

45 Which of the following businesses is **MOST LIKELY** to follow normal accounting rules (as opposed to hedge accounting rules) when reporting a financial instrument?

    A   A retailer

    B   A stockbroker

    C   An engineering company

    D   An IT company

46 **LINE Co is a German company whose functional currency is the euro (EUR).**

The directors of LINE Co decided in January 20X4 that the company will need to buy a piece of equipment from a US supplier in August 20X4 for USD 200,000.

As a result of being risk averse it wishes to hedge the risk that the cost of buying US dollars will rise and so enters into a forward contract to buy USD 200,000 in August 20X4 for the fixed sum of EUR 200,000. The fair value of this contract at inception is zero.

At the year end of 31 July 20X4 the euro has actually appreciated and the present value of USD 200,000 is EUR 190,000.

How should this be dealt with in the financial statements of LINE Co for the year ended 31 July 20X4?

    A   Record the value of the forward as EUR 200,000 and wait until the equipment is purchased before making any further entries to reflect any movement in its value

    B   No entries yet, because the equipment hasn't yet been purchased

    C   Recognise a loss of EUR 10,000 in the statement of profit or loss for the year

    D   Recognise a loss of EUR 10,000 in other comprehensive income

47   Whim Co is a US company whose functional currency is the US dollar (USD). It has partly financed an investment of EUR 500m in a French company via the use of a loan of EUR 430m taken out on 1 January 20X1.

Exchange rates were as follows:

1 January 20X1
USD 1 = EUR 0.81

31 December 20X1
USD 1 = EUR 0.79

The above hedging arrangement satisfies the requirements for offset per IAS 39.

What is the percentage effectiveness of this net investment hedge at 31 December 20X1?

A   86%

B   98%

C   103%

D   116%

48   Nationwide Co owns inventories of 1,000 tons of copper which cost $10,000 on 1 December 20X5.

To minimise the risk of the price of copper falling, the entity entered into a futures contract to sell 1,000 tons of copper for $12,000 on 1 February 20X6.

At the year end of 31 December 20X5, the market value of the copper was $11 per ton and the futures price for delivery on 1 February 20X6 was $13 per ton.

Required:

Under the hedge accounting rules of IAS 39, what is the accounting entry at 31 December 20X5 to reflect the change in value of the copper?

A   Credit the statement of profit or loss with the gain of $1,000

B   Debit the statement of profit or loss with the loss of $1,000

C   Credit Other Comprehensive Income with the gain of $1,000

D   No entry is needed – gains should only be recognised when realized

49   The directors of Roon Co are considering a proposal to invest in a foreign subsidiary sometime over the next couple of years.

They are considering the possibility of hedge accounting, but they are not sure which accounting standard's provisions to follow.

If they intend to invest in the new subsidiary, and to fund the purchase with a foreign currency loan, which accounting standard's hedge accounting provisions should be followed?

A   IAS 39 irrespective of what date the hedge needs to be set up

B   IFRS 9 irrespective of what date the hedge needs to be set up

C   IAS 39 if the hedge needs to be set up before 1 January 2018

D   IFRS 9 if the hedge needs to be set up before 1 January 2018

50 Which of the following statements regarding futures and forward contracts is FALSE?

A Both forward contracts and futures contracts trade on an organised exchange

B Forwards require no cash transactions until the delivery date, while futures require a margin deposit when the position is opened

C Futures contracts are highly standardised

D Forwards have default risk

SYLLABUS SECTION B: FINANCING AND DIVIDEND DECISIONS

51 A company is trying to decide between raising equity or debt for a new project.

Which factor is most likely to influence the decision towards debt?

A Interest rates are rising

B Dividends have been increasing at 3% each year for the last few years

C Gearing is currently very low

D The company is expected to make a loss in the next year

52 All else equal, which of the following will help decrease a company's total debt to equity ratio?

A Lowering the dividend payout ratio

B Buying treasury bills

C Paying cash dividends to shareholders

D Converting long-term debt to short-term debt

53 An entity's target or optimal capital structure is consistent with which of the following?

A Minimum risk

B Minimum weighted average cost of capital

C Maximum earnings per share

D Minimum cost of debt

54 An entity's capital structure affects which of the following?

A default risk but not return on equity

B return on equity but not default risk

C return on equity and default risk

D neither return on equity nor default risk

55   **Which of the following factors might cause an entity to increase the debt in its capital structure?**

   A   An increase in the corporate income tax rate

   B   Increased economic uncertainty

   C   An increase in the base rate of interest

   D   An increase in the price/earnings ratio

56   **Which THREE of the following are key assumptions of Modigliani and Miller's 1963 gearing theory?**

   A   Investors prefer corporate gearing to personal gearing

   B   Companies do pay tax

   C   There are no transaction costs

   D   The capital market is efficient at the semi-strong level

   E   Equity is risk free

   F   Cost of debt stays constant at all levels of gearing

57   **Modigliani and Miller's 1963 gearing theory concludes that:**

   A   The cost of capital is unaffected by the gearing level

   B   The cost of capital reduces as the gearing level increases

   C   The cost of capital increases as the gearing level increases

   D   There is an optimum gearing level at which the cost of capital is minimised

   E   There is an optimum gearing level at which the cost of capital is maximised

58   **The traditional view of gearing concludes that:**

   A   The value of the company reduces as the gearing level increases

   B   The value of the company increases as the gearing level increases

   C   The value of the company is unaffected by the gearing level

   D   There is an optimum gearing level at which the value of the company is maximised

   E   There is an optimum gearing level at which the value of the company is minimised

59   **XX Co is a geared company whose equity has a market value of $1,350 million and debt has a market value of $420 million.**

XX Co plans to issue $200 million of new shares, and to use the funds raised to pay off some of the debt.

XX Co currently has a cost of equity of 13.5%, and YY Co (an equivalent ungeared company operating in the same business sector as XX Co) has a cost of equity of 12.8%.

XX Co's WACC is currently 11.9% and the tax rate is 30%.

According to Modigliani and Miller's theory with tax, XX Co's WACC will move to:

A $$12.3\% = 12.8\% \times \left[1 - \left(\frac{0.30 \times 220}{1,770} \right) \right]$$

B $$12.9\% = 13.5\% \times \left[1 - \left(\frac{0.30 \times 220}{1,570} \right) \right]$$

C $$12.3\% = 12.8\% \times \left[1 - \left(\frac{0.30 \times 220}{1,570} \right) \right]$$

D $$13.0\% = 13.5\% \times \left[1 - \left(\frac{0.30 \times 220}{1,770} \right) \right]$$

60   **ZZZ is an ungeared company with a cost of equity of 10%. It is considering issuing some bonds, so that its gearing level will be 20% debt and 80% equity. The bonds will pay a coupon rate of 5%, and the yield required by the lenders will be 6%.**

If ZZZ pays tax at 25%, according to Modigliani and Miller's theory with tax, ZZZ's cost of equity will move to:

A $$11.25\% = 10\% + [(10\% - 5\%) \times (20/80)]$$

B $$10.75\% = 10\% + [(10\% - 6\%) \times (15/80)]$$

C $$10.94\% = 10\% + [(10\% - 5\%) \times (15/80)]$$

D $$11.00\% = 10\% + [(10\% - 6\%) \times (20/80)]$$

61 **Monty is an all-equity financed company with a cost of equity of 15%.**

The directors of Monty are proposing to raise $20 million to invest in a new project. This investment will carry similar risk to Monty's current business. It is proposed that the investment will be financed by either

- a rights issue of shares, or
- an issue of an undated bond carrying 6% interest pre-tax (this rate is deemed to reflect the returns required by the market for the risk and duration of the bond).

Earnings for Monty are forecast to be $30 million in the first year after the new investment. Subsequently, earnings are expected to remain at a constant level each year.

The corporate income tax rate is 20%. This is not expected to change.

According to Modigliani and Miller's theory with tax, the value of Monty's EQUITY if it issues the bond and undertakes this project will be:

A $204 million

B $200 million

C $184 million

D $180 million

62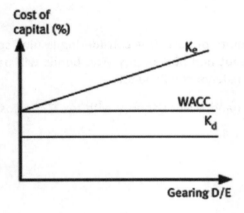

According to Modigliani and Miller's 1958 model of capital market efficiency, why is the cost of debt (Kd) lower than the cost of equity (Ke)?

A   Interest is received more regularly than dividends

B   Dividend tax credits are received by investors

C   Interest returns are more reliable than dividends

D   Interest is tax deductible

63   **C Co is identical in all operating and risk characteristics to D Co, but their capital structures differ:**

C Co: $72 million equity only

D Co: $36.2 million debt, 10 million shares

The tax rate is 33%.

What is the value of D Co's equity per share?

A $47.746 million

B $3.58

C $4.77

D $7.20

64   **A Co is identical in all operating and risk characteristics to B Co, but their capital structures differ.**

B Co is financed only by equity, currently valued at $37.2 million.

A Co has equity : debt 2:1 as its capital structure.

A Co's pre-tax cost of debt is 7.5%, and B Co's cost of equity is 17.5%.

A Co and B Co both operate in a country where tax is payable at 33%.

What is the cost of equity for A Co (to 2 decimal places)?

A   20.85%

B   13.06%

C   22.50%

D   7.77%

65   **According to Modigliani and Miller the cost of equity will always fall with decreased gearing because:**

A   The firm is less likely to go bankrupt

B   Debt is allowable against tax

C   The return to shareholders becomes less variable

D   The tax shield on debt increases the value of the shareholders' equity

66 Which one of the following diagrams is consistent with the so-called 'traditional view' of gearing often held in contrast with the views of Modigliani and Miller?

A

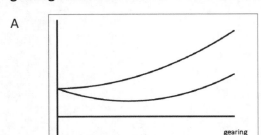

B

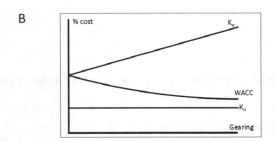

C

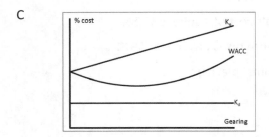

D

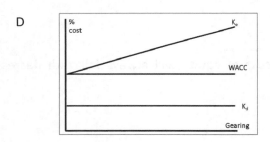

67 Cork currently has a gearing ratio of 20% (based on market values and measured as debt/ (debt + equity) and a WACC of 9.4%. The corporation tax rate is 30%.

Calculate, using Modigliani and Miller's theory with tax, the theoretical WACC for Cork if gearing were to be increased to 40%.

Enter your answer as a percentage to one decimal place

_____(INSERT CORRECT FIGURE IN THE BOX)

68   Davis is an all equity financed company with a market value of $60m and a cost of capital of 15% per annum. The corporation tax rate is 30%.

If the company repurchases $20m of equity and replaces it with 6% undated bonds, what will be the company's new WACC?

A   11.4%

B   12.0%

C   13.5%

D   13.6%

69   Lallana is an all equity financed company with an ungeared cost of equity of 15%. They have been advised that if the company were to issue debt and use the funds to repurchase shares it would lower the company's WACC. The corporation tax rate is 30%.

If the Board would like to reduce WACC by 1%, what would be the required gearing ratio (measured as debt/(debt + equity) using market values) to achieve this?

Enter your answer as a percentage to two decimal places

_____(INSERT CORRECT FIGURE IN THE BOX)

70   Schneiderlin currently has a gearing ratio of 20% (based on market values and measured as debt/(debt + equity) and a WACC of 9.4%. The corporation tax rate is 30%.

Calculate, using Modigliani and Miller's theory with tax, the relative percentage change in WACC for Schneiderlin plc if gearing were to be increased to 40%.

Enter your answer as a percentage to one decimal place

_____(INSERT CORRECT FIGURE IN THE BOX)

71   Wanyama has 20m equity shares in issue trading at 260 cents per share and an 8% bank loan of $8m. The corporation tax rate is 30%. The Board are considering issuing more shares in order to pay off the bank loan but are unsure of the impact it will have on the company's WACC. The company's cost of equity is currently 14%.

Calculate the new WACC if the Board's proposal goes ahead.

_____(INSERT CORRECT FIGURE IN THE BOX)

72

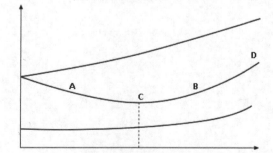

Traditional model of capital structure theory

Consider the Weighted Average Cost of Capital (WACC) line above.

In the context of a typical manufacturing company, what is represented by each of the 4 points labelled A, B, C and D? Match one correct letter to each statement below.

	Insert letter
Wealth maximising capital structure	
Conservative capital structure	
Aggressive capital structure	
Theoretical capital structure	

73   **Which of the following diagrams is the closest illustration of the situation described in Modigliani and Miller's 1963 with tax hypothesis, if gearing is measured by the ratio of debt to equity?**

A

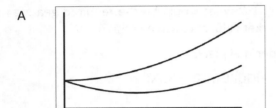

B

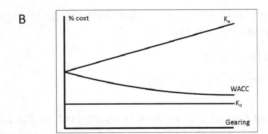

C

D

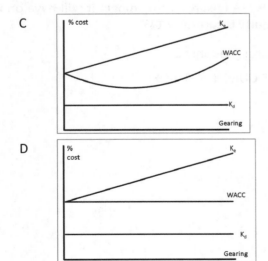

74   In relation to Modigliani and Miller's 1963 with tax hypothesis, which of the following claims is NOT valid?

    A   The cost of equity is directly proportional to the ratio of debt to equity

    B   Investors are indifferent between personal and corporate gearing

    C   Investors and companies can borrow at the same rate of interest

    D   Capital structure has no effect on the WACC or the value of the entity

75   YrElen Co is currently all equity financed and has a cost of capital of 15%. It is considering changing its capital structure by issuing, at par, long dated bonds with a coupon rate of 5%. It plans to have a debt to equity ratio of 1 to 4. The company pays tax at 20%.

What will be the resultant Weighted Average Cost of Capital (WACC)?

_____(INSERT CORRECT FIGURE IN THE BOX, rounded to 1 decimal place of a % point)

76   Ygarn Co is currently financed by $100 million of equity shares and $40 million of debt. Its cost of equity is 14% and the pre-tax cost of debt is 8%. It pays tax at a rate of 20%.

What would the cost of equity change to if the company changed its debt to equity ratio to 60%?

_____(INSERT CORRECT FIGURE IN THE BOX, rounded to 1 decimal place of a % point)

77   GlyderFawr Co is currently all equity financed with 10 million shares in issue. The shares have a current market value of $9.50 each. The company is considering issuing $20 million of debt and using the proceeds to re-purchase some of its own equity shares (at market value). It pays corporation tax at 20%

What would be the market value, per share, of the remaining equity shares?

_____(INSERT CORRECT FIGURE IN THE BOX, in $ to 2 decimal places)

78   Which of the following is a difference between primary and secondary capital markets?

    A   Both primary and secondary markets relate to where shares and bonds trade after their initial offering

    B   Secondary capital markets relate to the sale of new issues of bonds, preference shares, and ordinary shares, while primary capital markets are where securities trade after their initial offering

    C   Primary capital markets relate to the sale of new issues of bonds, preference shares, and ordinary shares, while secondary capital markets are where securities trade after their initial offering.

    D   Primary markets are where shares trade while secondary markets are where bonds trade

79 **The interest rate risk of a bond is the:**

    A   risk related to the possibility of bankruptcy of the bond's issuer

    B   unsystematic risk caused by factors unique in the bond

    C   risk related to the possibility of bankruptcy of the bond's issuer, that arises from the uncertainty of the bond's return caused by the change in interest rates

    D   risk that arises from the uncertainty about the bond's return caused by changes in interest rates over time

80 **If Brewer Corporation's bonds are currently yielding 8% in the marketplace, why would the entity's cost of debt be lower?**

    A   Additional debt can be issued more cheaply than the original debt

    B   Market interest rates have increased

    C   There should be no difference; cost of debt is the same as the bonds' market yield

    D   Interest is deductible for tax purposes

81 **Which of a firm's sources of new capital usually has the lowest after-tax cost?**

    A   Preference shares

    B   Ordinary shares

    C   Mezzanine debt

    D   Bonds

82 **Enter the correct word from the choices given:**

Company X has two covenants attached to its borrowings:

- The interest cover ratio must be _____ **(higher/lower)** than 3

- The ratio of net debt to EBITDA must be _____ **(higher/lower)** than 3

83 **A company has issued tradeable bonds which have a covenant attached. The covenant does not allow the gearing ratio (as measured by debt divided by equity, calculated on market values) to exceed 45%. If the covenant is breached, then the bonds become immediately re-payable.**

This morning, the share price fell to $1.75. The company has 1m shares in issue. It also has $0.4m of bank loans and $0.5m (nominal) of bonds. The bonds are currently trading at $88 per $100 nominal.

Has the covenant been breached and if so, what action must be taken immediately to try to bring it back into line to avoid having to repay the bonds?

    A   Covenant breached – yes. Release news about lucrative, new projects

    B   Covenant breached – yes. Borrow more from the bank to increase liquidity

    C   Covenant breached – yes. Launch a share re-purchase scheme

    D   Covenant breached – no. No action required

84 Robb Co has issued convertible bonds a few years ago. A holder of a bond has the option of converting to 28 shares or receiving $100 cash per bond on the redemption date.

The current (1 January 20X1) share price is $3.20 and this is expected to grow at 3% per annum.

At which date would conversion be worthwhile?

A   31 December 20X1

B   31 December 20X2

C   31 December 20X3

D   31 December 20X4

85 Which of the following statements regarding subordinated debt is NOT correct?

A   In the case of default, shareholders would be paid out before subordinated debt holders

B   In case of default, creditors with subordinated debt wouldn't get paid out until after the senior debt holders are paid

C   Subordinated debt takes a higher ranking than ordinary shareholders

D   Subordinated debt is a debt which has a lower ranking than senior debt

86 An operating lease is best defined by which statement?

A   A method of raising finance to pay for an asset

B   A contract that transfers substantially all the risks and rewards of ownership to the lessee

C   A contract which allows the transfer of the asset to the lessee at the end of the lease term

D   A contract that allows the use of an asset but does not convey rights of ownership

87 Sansa Co is looking to acquire a new piece of machinery. If buying, the machine will cost $1m and will attract capital allowances on a reducing balance basis at 25% per annum. The life of the machine is expected to be four years with no residual value. If it is leased, the lease payments will be $275,000 in advance each year.

Sansa Co can borrow from its bank at 8.57% per annum and pays tax at 30% one year in arrears. If leasing, the full lease payment will qualify for tax relief.

What is the present value of the lease payments (to the nearest '000)?

A   ($759,000)

B   ($740,000)

C   ($502,000)

D $11,000

88 Company S is considering acquiring an asset which will cost $450,000 to purchase outright. However S is exploring a lease arrangement. The lessor will charge $120,000 per annum in arrears for four years. Tax relief is available in the year in which profits are earned at 30%. Only the interest element of the lease payment will attract tax relief.

Using the sum of the digits method, what is the tax relief on the interest paid in year 3?

A $6,000

B $2,700

C $1,800

D $900

89 **Bran Co is considering whether to lease or buy an asset.**

The financial controller has been researching the costs involved with borrowing from the bank to buy the asset outright. The bank will charge interest at 7.14% per annum. The asset will cost $500,000 and will attract tax allowable depreciation on a straight line basis over five years, which is the useful economic life of the asset. There is no residual value.

Bran Co is subject to corporation tax at 30%, payable in the year in which the profit is earned.

To the nearest $000, what is the NPV of the buy option?

_____(INSERT CORRECT FIGURE IN THE BOX)

90 When deciding between leasing or borrowing to acquire an asset, the discount rate usually used in the net present value calculations for the lease versus buy decision should be:

A   The company's WACC

B   The company's post-tax cost of borrowing

C   The company's pre-tax cost of borrowing

D   The implied interest rate in the lease payments

91 **Company A would like to take out a variable rate loan for a new project. Company B also has a new project but would like to take out a fixed rate loan in order to have certainty over interest payments.**

Company A has been quoted a fixed rate of 7% and a variable rate of LIBOR+4%. Company B has been quoted a fixed rate of 6% and a variable rate of LIBOR+2% as it has a higher credit rating than A.

If they enter into a swap arrangement, what effective rate will each end up paying?

A	Co A 7%		Co B	LIBOR+2%
B	Co A LIBOR+4%		Co B	6%
C	Co A LIBOR+2%		Co B	7%
D	Co A LIBOR+3.5%		Co B	5.5%

92 **Which THREE of the following are advantages of using interest rate swaps?**

A   to manage fixed and floating rate debt profiles without having to change underlying borrowing

B   to hedge against variations in interest on floating rate debt

C   to protect the fair value of floating rate debt instruments

D   to obtain cheaper finance

93 **DD Co has a floating rate borrowing, whose interest rate is LIBOR + 1.5%.**

The directors are concerned that interest rates are forecast to rise, so they have approached the bank to discuss the possibility of entering an interest rate swap.

The bank has quoted a swap rate of 5% against LIBOR.

If DD Co enters the swap arrangement, what net interest rate will it pay?

A   LIBOR + 5%

B   5%

C   6.5%

D   3.5%

94 **V Co is a company whose directors are considering an Initial Public Offering (IPO) of shares.**

The directors are hoping to generate a large amount of cash for the company, so they intend to appoint an advisor to organise the IPO.

Who should the directors appoint to organise the IPO?

A   an underwriter

B   a stockbroker

C   an investment bank

D   an institutional investor

95 **A company makes a 1 for 5 rights issue at a price of $3.50. The cum-rights price is $5.**

What is the theoretical ex-rights price?

A $3.75

B $4.25

C $4.70

D $4.75

96   A company currently has 15 million $1 shares in issue with a market value of $5 per share. The company wishes to raise new funds using a 1 for 3 rights issue.

If the theoretical ex rights price per share turns out to be $4.80, how much new finance was raised?

A $21 million

B $24 million

C $207 million

D $213 million

97   A listed company makes a rights issue.

Which of the following rankings of prices is most valid?

A   Ex rights price < Cum rights price < Issue price

B   Issue price < Cum rights price < Ex rights price

C   Cum rights price < Ex rights price < Issue price

D   Issue price < Ex rights price < Cum rights price

98   The following describes the terms of a rights issue for Ray Co:

Market price = $3; discount to market price of 10%; two new shares offered per five existing ones held.

What is the theoretical ex-rights price (TERP)?

A $2.79

B $2.91

C $2.95

D $3.09

99   The main reason for discounting a rights issue is:

A   To make the shares attractive to shareholders

B   To counteract the dilution of owner's equity

C   To safeguard against the risk of a fall in market price during the offer period

D   To return value to existing shareholders

100   An all equity financed company is about to raise the finance for a new project by an issue of ordinary shares to the general public. The new project has a positive Net Present Value (NPV).

If all the gain from the new project is to go to the existing shareholders, which of the following statements about the issue price (per share) of the new shares is true?

A   It must be equal to the nominal value of the share issued

B   It must be equal to the current market value of an existing share

C   It must be at a discount to the current market value of an existing share

D   It must be greater than the current market value of an existing share

101 **Snowdon Co is financed entirely by equity comprising 10 million ordinary shares with a current market value of $5 per share. It is planning to make an issue of new ordinary shares to the general public in order to raise the funds to invest in a new project which will cost $5.28 million, and will give a positive NPV of $1.885 million. The issue will be priced at a 4% discount to the current share price.**

What (to the nearest $) will be the total gain accruing to the existing shareholders?

_____(INSERT CORRECT FIGURE IN THE BOX)

102 **CribGoch Co is financed entirely by equity comprising 10 million ordinary shares with a current market value of $5 per share.**

It is planning to make an issue of new ordinary shares to the general public in order to raise the funds to invest in a new project which will cost $5.28 million, and will give a positive NPV of $2.44 million.

The issue will be priced at a 4% discount to the current share price.

What percentage (to 2 decimal places) of the total gain will go to the new shareholders?

_____(INSERT CORRECT FIGURE IN THE BOX)

103 **Tryfan Co intends to invest $8 million in a new project with an NPV of $3 million. The company is currently financed entirely by 30 million shares with a market value of $2.50 per share. The funds for the new project will be raised by issuing new ordinary shares to a private investor.**

What price should the new shares be issued at if all the gain is to go to the existing shareholders?

_____(INSERT CORRECT FIGURE IN THE BOX, in $ to 2 decimal places)

104 **GlyderFach Co is financed entirely by equity comprising 20 million ordinary shares with a current market value of $3.50 per share. It is planning to make an issue of new ordinary shares to the general public at a discount of 10% to the current market price in order to raise the funds to invest in a new project. The new project will cost $2.835 million and generates a positive Net Present Value of $1.151 million.**

What is the gain per share for the new investors?

_____(INSERT CORRECT FIGURE IN THE BOX, in $ to 2 decimal places)

105 **Which of the following is the best statement of the conclusion of Modigliani and Miller on the relevance of dividend policy?**

A   All shareholders are indifferent between receiving dividend income and capital gains

B   Increase in retentions results in a higher growth rate

C   The value of the shareholders' equity is determined solely by the firm's investment selection criteria

D   Discounting the dividends is not an appropriate way to value the firm's equity

106 Some companies have a long-term dividend policy of paying out no dividends. A notable example has been Microsoft, the US software corporation.

Which of the following is the weakest and least likely reason for justifying a no-dividend policy over the long term?

A   Retained profits are a cheaper source of new finance than raising new capital in the markets

B   The tax treatment of capital gains is more favourable than the tax treatment of dividends

C   Shareholders needing cash can sell shares in the stock market at any time, and so do not need dividends

D   The company is a growth company and investors buying shares in the company recognise that all profits will be reinvested for growth

107 According to Modigliani and Miller's dividend irrelevancy theory, investors are indifferent as to whether they receive a dividend or capital growth in their share value as they can manufacture their own dividend by selling shares.

Why may an investor disagree with this theory? Choose 3 from the following 5.

A   Transaction costs may apply when selling shares

B   Tax planning will be affected

C   Share price will fall if no dividends are paid

D   The investor is reliant on the cash dividend

E   The investor's ability to influence management will be reduced

108 According to Modigliani and Miller's 1963 'with tax' model, why are interest costs cheaper for a company to finance than dividend costs? Select 2 of the following

A   Dividends are paid out of post-tax earnings

B   Debt is secured on specific assets

C   Interest returns are guaranteed

D   Dividends can be reduced if company performance is weak

E   Lower transaction costs

109 Cazorla Co has paid a reliable dividend in recent years. It is considering reducing its dividend to conserve cash.

Cazorla Co's share price is likely to fall due to which 3 of the following?

A   Disappointed investors selling shares

B   Low returns earned on conserved cash

C   Poor performance of the business relative to other companies

D   Investors selling shares to replace lost dividends

E   Negative market perception of company performance

110   **Enter the correct word from the choices given:**

Company X is planning on _____**(increasing/decreasing)** its dividend, but is concerned that the share price will fall.

This demonstrates the _____**(signalling/clientele)** effect.

111   **Popov Co currently has 10 million $0.50 ordinary shares in issue, trading at $1.93.**

A proposed new project is expected to have a net present value of $6 million and requires an initial investment of $5 million. The project's internal rate of return is expected to be 9%.

If the market is efficient and the share price moves to reflect this information on the day that the project is announced, what is the theoretical movement in the share price on that day?

A $0.60 increase

B $0.10 increase

C $0.50 decrease

D   No change

112   **PP Co made an operating profit of $305,000 last year, and its directors are considering issuing £500,000 of new secured bonds at their par value of $100. The coupon rate will be 2.5%.**

PP Co is a listed company. It currently has 1 million $0.50 shares in issue, trading at $0.95, and 10,000, 4% coupon bonds with par value $100 and market value $95.

What will be the interest cover of PP Co in the year after the bonds are issued, on the assumption that operating profits will stay constant?

A   5.8

B   6.0

C   8.1

D   18.5

113 **Lung Co has a debt covenant that requires its gearing ratio (measured as debt/(debt + equity) using market values) to be less than 35%, and its interest cover to be greater than 2.2**

Extracts from its recent financial statements show that it has 200,000 $1 shares in issue and it has a 9% interest bank loan of $100,000. It made a profit before interest and tax last year of $25,000.

The current share price is $1.30 per share.

The directors of Lung Co are considering borrowing an extra $40,000 from the bank as a secured loan at an interest rate of 5% per annum.

Annual profits are expected to stay constant, but the share price is expected to fall to $1.25 per share to reflect the shareholders' perception of increased financial risk.

Assuming the new finance is raised, which of the following shows Grass Co's position with regard to its debt covenant:

	Gearing	Interest cover
A	MET	MET
B	FAILED	MET
C	FAILED	FAILED
D	MET	FAILED

114 **Na Co currently has a cash balance of $5 million and earnings per share of $0.30.**

It has 6 million $0.25 shares in issue, but the directors are planning to repurchase 1 million of these shares at a price of $0.40 each.

What will be the cash balance and the earnings per share (EPS) after the share repurchase?

	Cash	EPS
A	$3.0 million	$0.36
B	$4.6 million	$0.36
C	$3.0 million	$0.25
D	$4.6 million	$0.25

115 **The directors of Strange Co are considering using either a 6% interest bank loan, or issuing 250,000 ordinary shares at a price of $4, to raise necessary funds for expansion.**

The expansion will generate $300,000 of extra operating profit each year.

Strange Co pays tax at 30%.

Key investor ratios for Strange Co are currently as follows:

Interest cover = (Earnings before interest and tax/Interest payable) = $1,300,000/$280,000 = 4.6 times

Earnings per share (EPS) = (Profit after tax/No. of shares) = $714,000/1,000,000 = $0.714

Gearing = (debt/equity) = $4m/$7m = 57.1%

Which TWO of the following statements are correct?

A   Gearing falls when using equity and rises when using debt

B   EPS increases more by using debt

C   Equity reduces gearing and gives the best EPS

D   EPS and interest cover both worsen using debt

E   Interest cover is reduced using either source of finance

116 **After several years of growth, Goose Co has accumulated a cash pile of $10 million. The directors have decided to repurchase some of the company's shares at market value in order to return this cash pile to the shareholders.**

Goose Co has 40 million $1 shares in issue, trading at $3.14. It also has $50 million of bonds in issue, trading at $99 per cent.

What will be the gearing level of Goose Co after the share repurchase? (measured as debt/(debt + equity) using market values)

A   26.7%

B   28.3%

C   30.0%

D   62.5%

117 **The directors of Singh Co are considering raising $500,000 in order to undertake a new project. It is expected that the new project will cause earnings to rise by $50,000 each year. Singh Co has 2 million $0.50 shares in issue, which are currently trading at $0.90. Singh Co's P/E ratio is 8.55.**

If Singh Co uses a 1 for 2 rights issue to raise the finance, what is the expected earnings per share (EPS) of Singh Co after the finance has been raised and the project undertaken?

A $0.500

B $0.105

C $0.087

D $0.050

118 Tide Co is a listed company. Its $1 ordinary shares are quoted on the local stock exchange.

The Board of Tide Co is aware that the market is expecting Tide Co to pay a dividend of $100m to be paid at the year end, but in order to fund the investment in an important new project, the Board is considering offering a scrip dividend of 1 share for every 10 shares held instead of a cash dividend.

Profit after tax and interest is forecast to be $290 million in the current financial year, and Tide Co's equity comprises:

Ordinary share capital ($1 shares) $1,000m

Reserves $400m

Tide Co's share price is $1.65 per share.

What is the expected share price of Tide Co after the scrip dividend has been issued? (to 2 decimal places)

A $1.82

B $1.65

C $1.50

D $0.17

119 UU Co is considering raising $3 million of new long term debt finance to fund the acquisition of Ping Co.

Ping Co is considered to have a value to UU Co of $3.6 million. UU Co's most recent statement of financial position shows long term borrowings of $6.2 million, share capital ($1 shares) of $4 million and accumulated reserves of $6.1 million. The current market share price for UU Co is $3.08 per share.

What will be the gearing ratio – measured as (debt/(debt + equity)) at book value – after the acquisition?

A   47.7%

B   46.2%

C   42.8%

D   41.6%

120   Statement of financial position for Shadows Co

	$m
Non-current assets (total)	28.0
Current assets (total)	25.0
TOTAL ASSETS	53.0
Equity and Liabilities	
Ordinary share capital	20.0
Ordinary share premium	4.0
Preference share capital (irredeemable)	5.0
Reserves	6.0
Non-current liabilities	
10% bonds	10.0
Current liabilities	
Trade creditors	3.0
Bank overdraft	5.0
TOTAL EQUITY & LIABILITIES	53.0

Shadows Co statement of profit or loss extract	$m
Operating profit (PBIT)	8.3
Finance charges	(1.0)
Profit before tax (PBT)	7.3
Tax @ 30%	(2.2)
Net profit	5.1

Shadows Co is considering raising additional debt finance of $8m. The interest rate on the new debt will be 8% per annum. Operating profit is expected to stay constant after the new finance has been raised.

What will be the interest cover and the capital gearing ratio (measured as debt/(debt + equity) at book value) for Shadows Co after the new finance has been raised?

A   Interest cover 5.06, gearing 39.7%

B   Interest cover 5.06, gearing 53.5%

C   Interest cover 12.97, gearing 39.7%

D   Interest cover 12.97, gearing 53.5%

SYLLABUS SECTION C: CORPORATE FINANCE

121   **Which THREE of the following reasons are often given as reasons for a spin-off?**

    A   to reduce the risk of a takeover bid for the core entity

    B   to divest of a less profitable business unit if an acceptable offer is received

    C   to generate cash in a time of crisis

    D   to allow investors to identify the true value of a business that was hidden within a large conglomerate

    E   to give a clearer management structure

122   **Asset stripping is a common reason given by entities as why they wish to buy a target company.**

    What is asset stripping?

    A   Buying a small percentage of the share capital of the target company

    B   Purchasing all of the share capital of the target company and also settling the entity's debts

    C   Buying all the share capital of the business and then selling off the assets

    D   Purchasing the assets of a target company on a piecemeal basis

123   **Mr S and Mrs Q are the managers of Spring Co, an underperforming subsidiary of Season Co. They are in the process of putting together a bid to use a management buyout (MBO) to take control of Spring Co by buying the company from Season Co.**

    The plan is that the managers themselves will invest 20% of the necessary funds and the other 80% will be provided by a venture capitalist and a bank. Over the next five years, if the MBO goes ahead and is successful, Mr S and Mrs Q plan to increase their stake incrementally by buying out the venture capitalist year by year.

    Which THREE of the following reasons could explain why Spring Co might be more successful after the MBO?

    A   Greater motivation for the managers to succeed

    B   Better objectives set by managers who understand the business better

    C   Greater economies of scale

    D   More flexibility to change without having to wait for parent company approval

    E   No need to pay dividends to Season Co

124 Venture capitalists often provide finance to help with management buyouts.

Which of the following reasons best explains why management buyouts are generally structured so that the venture capital finance is a mixture of equity and debt?

A   Because the Traditional View of gearing suggests that the optimum financing structure is a mix of debt and equity

B   Because 100% debt finance would be too risky

C   Because 100% equity finance means that the entity forgoes tax relief on debt interest

D   Because the venture capitalist wants some equity finance to provide a high rate of return, but not so much that it takes control of the company

125 If a company believes that after acquiring another company, it will be in a better position to access low cost debt finance, this would be categorised as:

A   a synergy of complementary resources

B   an economy of scale

C   an economy of vertical integration

D   bootstrapping

126 Shaw Inc is a software development business and is based in the USA. Luke Co is a service business that writes bespoke computer programs for its clients. It is based in the UK.

Luke Co has made an offer to buy Shaw Inc.

What would this type of acquisition be best described as?

A   Horizontal Integration

B   Portfolio Acquisition

C   Vertical Integration

D   None of the above

127 What is a reverse takeover?

A   The buyer pulls out of the purchase of the vendor business at the eleventh hour

B   The acquisition of a larger company by a smaller company

C   Certain assets of an entity are hived off to a new subsidiary company and then this subsidiary is sold off

D   A company sells a small part of its business to selective members of its management team

128 Herra Inc is an engineering business making parts for the car industry. Anders Co is a small family-owned entity that retails car parts for local car mechanics.

Herra has made an offer to buy Anders.

What would this type of acquisition be best described as?

A   Horizontal Integration

B   Portfolio Acquisition

C   Vertical Integration

D   None of the above

129 Many countries have set up regulators (for example the UK has The Competition and Markets Authority (CMA)) to oversee merger and acquisition activity.

What is the main role of such regulators?

A   To ensure that the buyer and seller arrive at a fair price for the vendor business

B   To mediate between the buyer and seller when there is a hostile take-over

C   To protect relevant stakeholders as the combined buyer and seller may wield monopoly power

D   To advise the government on merger and acquisition law

130 Nuruk Inc intends to launch a hostile takeover bid for Penn Co. The companies are direct competitors. The directors of Penn Co have heard rumours that the bid is about to be made, but they don't think that a takeover by Nuruk Inc would be in the best interests of Penn Co's shareholders.

Which of the following defence strategies could be used by Penn Co?

A   Make a counter bid

B   Find a white knight

C   Refer the bid to the competition authorities

D   Change the Articles of Association to require a greater proportion of shareholders (super majority) to vote to accept any bid

131 Which TWO of the following reasons could be used as a justification for a spin-off?

A   To raise cash for further investment

B   To eliminate diseconomies of scale

C   To pay excess cash back to shareholders

D   To comply with a legal or regulatory requirement

E   To enable the managers of a business unit to take control of their business

132 **King Co is the subject of a rumoured takeover from Queen Co, although no firm offer has yet been made.**

Which THREE of the following strategic defence methods could be used by the directors of King Co in this situation?

A   White knight

B   Pacman

C   Appeal to the shareholders to reject any forthcoming offer

D   Poison pill

E   Super majority

133 **Which of the following benefits generated from a merger of two independent entities would NOT be classified as a synergy from operating economies?**

A   an economy of scale

B   bootstrapping

C   an economy of vertical integration

D   complementary resources

134 **Which of the following is the BEST definition of bootstrapping?**

A   an increase in value generated when an entity with a low P/E ratio acquires an entity with a higher P/E ratio

B   an increase in value generated when an entity with a high P/E ratio acquires an entity with a lower P/E ratio

C   the synergy created by merging the activities of two similar sized entities

D   the gains made by a target entity's shareholders during the process of acquisition

135 **A listed company, Noon Co, is in negotiations with an unlisted company, Hall Co, regarding a possible takeover of the entire equity capital of the company.**

Noon Co's directors have offered to purchase Hall Co's shares at a price that is 20% higher than the price charged when a parcel of 10% of Hall Co's shares was sold last month.

Which of the following reasons is LEAST likely to explain why Noon Co has offered to pay a high price for the Hall Co shares?

A   Noon Co expects there to be significant synergistic gains from the acquisition

B   Noon Co understands that a premium will have to be paid when acquiring a controlling interest

C   Noon Co has used a different method of business valuation from the one used when the 10% parcel of shares was valued

D   Noon Co thinks that some of Hall Co's shareholders (especially the new shareholder who bought the 10% holding recently) may be unwilling to sell unless a significant premium is offered

136   Country T and Country V are separated by sea but linked by a rail tunnel.

They have different currencies (T$ and V$ respectively) but are part of the same Trade Group which promotes free trade between its members and has authority over membership countries in matters relating to competition.

TNL is a public listed company, based in Country T, which owns and operates the rail link between Country T and Country V. Trains that travel through the tunnel carry passengers, cars and other vehicles such as trucks.

There is strong price competition between TNL and two independent ferry companies, TT and VV which are based in Countries T and V respectively. Prices are generally low for travel by ferry since ferries are less convenient as they operate less frequently and have longer journey times than the rail tunnel link. TT has incurred losses in the past two years.

The board of TNL has approached ferry company TT with a view to acquiring it.

The directors of TT are opposed to the bid and have referred the bid to the regional competition authorities of both Country T and the Trade Group.

Which THREE of the following are likely reasons for TNL wanting to acquire TT?

A   To obtain synergies of vertical integration

B   To increase market power

C   To obtain tax relief

D   To increase market share

E   Diversification of risk

137   Muller Co is a sportwear manufacturer. It has just made a bid for Biglia Co, a similar company based in a different country.

Both companies are listed on their respective country's stock exchanges and the day the bid was announced, the share prices of both companies rose.

Which of the following is NOT a sensible explanation as to why this happened?

A   The stock markets are strongly efficient

B   Investors believe that the takeover will increase their wealth

C   The market believes that synergy will be generated as a consequence of the takeover

D   Biglia Co and Muller Co are perceived as being a good strategic fit

138   The competition authorities have been asked to investigate the takeover of Lager Co, a café-bar company, by a larger company Bitter Co.

Which of the following is LEAST likely to be the outcome of the investigation?

A   The takeover is allowed to proceed, subject to a higher payment being made by Bitter Co to the Lager Co shareholders

B   The takeover is blocked

C   The takeover is allowed to proceed

D   The takeover is allowed to proceed, subject to a limit on the number of retail outlets that the combined entity can own

139 **Gina Co is selling off an underperforming, loss making part of its business called JJ Co. Tommy Co has made a bid for JJ Co. The directors of Tommy Co intend merging JJ Co with an existing part of the Tommy Co business and expect the newly merged business unit to be profitable and successful.**

Which of the following reasons is LEAST likely to explain why Tommy Co will be able to generate more profits from this business unit than Gina Co could?

A   Synergies will be generated between Tommy Co and JJ Co

B   Tommy Co has more experienced managers than Gina Co has

C   JJ Co has a better strategic fit with Tommy Co than with Gina Co

D   Tommy Co has a higher cost of capital than Gina Co

140 **Country T and Country V are separated by sea but linked by a rail tunnel.**

They have different currencies (T$ and V$ respectively) but are part of the same Trade Group which promotes free trade between its members and has authority over membership countries in matters relating to competition.

TNL is a public listed company, based in Country T, which owns and operates the rail link between Country T and Country V. Trains that travel through the tunnel carry passengers, cars and other vehicles such as trucks.

There is strong price competition between TNL and two independent ferry companies, TT and VV which are based in Countries T and V respectively. Prices are generally low for travel by ferry since ferries are less convenient as they operate less frequently and have longer journey times than the rail tunnel link. TT has incurred losses in the past two years.

The board of TNL has approached ferry company TT with a view to acquiring it.

The directors of TT are opposed to the bid and have referred the bid to the regional competition authorities of both Country T and the Trade Group.

Which of the following is LEAST likely to be of concern to the competition authorities?

A   TNL and TT combined might be able to start a price war to force VV out of business

B   TT's directors are opposed to the bid

C   Prices for customers might rise after the takeover

D   The takeover might not be in the public interest

141 **An all equity company is just about to pay a dividend of $0.60 per share. The company confidently expects the dividend to grow at 10% a year. The company has estimated its cost of capital to be 13%.**

What would you expect the current quoted share price to be?

A $22.00

B $22.60

C $20.00

D $20.60

142 **Alpha Co has a P/E ratio of 16 and post-tax earnings of $200,000.**

Beta Co has a P/E ratio of 21 and post-tax earnings of $800,000.

Gamma Co has a P/E ratio of 20 and post-tax earnings of $600,000.

What is the rank order of the size of these companies, ranked by value? (largest first)

A Alpha, Beta, Gamma

B Alpha, Gamma, Beta

C Gamma, Alpha, Beta

D Gamma, Beta, Alpha

E Beta, Gamma, Alpha

F Beta, Alpha, Gamma

143 **GGG Co is intending to take over FFF Co.**

GGG Co has a P/E ratio of 10 and post-tax earnings of $5m, and FFF Co has a P/E ratio of 8 and post-tax earnings of $3m.

GGG's directors estimate that if they were to acquire FFF there would be annual synergies of $0.5m for the new combined company. Additionally they estimate that the P/E ratio of the new company would be 9.5.

On the basis of these estimates, what is the maximum that GGG should pay for the entire share capital of FFF?

A $24.00 million

B $30.75 million

C $33.25 million

D $80.75 million

144 **The most recent financial statements for Nye Co show the following:**

	$000
Interest	210
Investment in Non-Current Assets	378
Dividends	134
Operating Profit	879
Investment in Working Capital	143
Depreciation	167
Debt Repaid	100

The company pays tax on company profits at the rate of 22%.

What is Nye Co's free cash flow (to the nearest $000)?

A $68,000

B $168,000

C $332,000

D $335,000

145 **Which of the following correctly describes the discounted free cash flow method that can be used to value an entity's equity?**

A   Deduct interest and dividends in arriving at the forecast free cash flows and then discount the latter at the cost of equity

B   Discount the forecast free cash flows at the entity's WACC and then deduct the market value of the entity's debt

C   Forecast the free cash flows, without deducting taxation, and discount these at the entity's WACC

D   Deduct interest but not dividends in arriving at the forecast free cash flows and then discount the latter at the cost of equity

146 **Win Co wishes to ascertain the value of its equity. It has prepared the following schedule of forecast post-tax cash flows before financing charges:**

	Year 1	Year 2	Year 3	Year 4
$m	283	291	298	305

The forecast cash flows are expected to grow at rate of 3% per annum after year 4 into perpetuity. Win Co has a cost of equity of 15% and a WACC of 12%. The entity's debt is believed to be worth 30% of the total value of the entity.

What is the value of Win Co's equity?

A $891m

B $2,178m

C $2,536m

D $3,111m

147 **Eden Inc has recently published its latest accounts showing profit after tax of $23.12m, after deducting interest of $4.89m. Tax allowable depreciation was $4.55m and the company expects profits to grow at 5% per annum indefinitely.**

The company policy is to maintain its asset base by reinvesting cash to a value equal to the tax allowable depreciation. Eden has estimated its cost of equity at 12%, which is included in the company WACC of 10%

Assuming that profit after tax is the equivalent to cash flows, what is the value of the equity capital?

A $346.80m

B $485.52m

C $588.21m

D $683.76m

148 Tanu Inc has 1 million $0.50 par value shares in issue. It generated free cash flow of $1.5 million last year and expects this figure to grow by 4% per annum in the future.

Tanu Inc has a cost of equity of 14% and a WACC of 10%. It has $500,000 of bonds in issue, trading at $80 per $100.

What is the estimated value of a Tanu Inc share?

A $7.80

B $12.80

C $15.60

D $25.60

149 Company A and Company B operate in the same industry, but have different price earnings (P/E) ratios as follows:

	P/E ratio
Company A	8
Company B	15

Which of the following is the most probable explanation of the difference in the P/E ratios between the two companies?

A   Company B has a greater profit this year than Company A

B   Company B is higher risk than Company A

C   Company B has higher expected growth than Company A

D   Company B has higher gearing than Company A

150 A company has 70,000 issued shares at 50c per share which are currently trading for 204c.

The company paid $6,000 in dividends to ordinary shareholders and $2,000 to preference shareholders. Profit after taxation was $17,000 and $10,000 was paid in taxation.

What is the Price Earnings (P/E) ratio of the company?

A   5.3

B   8.4

C   9.5

D   15.8

151 A high P/E ratio is usually seen as an indication that:

A   The company's earnings are poor

B   The company is likely to grow

C   The share is over priced

D   The dividend is excessive

152 The published data for Sounders Inc shows:

Earnings per share   20 cents

Dividend cover   4

Dividend yield   2%

What is the current price of Sounders Inc's ordinary shares?

A   25 cents

B   80 cents

C   160 cents

D   250 cents

153 The following data is available for Pop Inc:

P/E ratio: 10

Dividend cover: 4 times

Share capital: $2 million in 25c shares

The dividend is 2c per share

What is the total market price of Pop Inc?

A $1.6 million

B $6.4 million

C $8 million

D $64 million

154 Ayai is a company listed on its local stock exchange. An extract from the company's latest accounts shows:

	$000
25 cents ordinary share capital	500
Share premium	1,050
$1 preference shares	3,200
Income reserves	2,135
6.25% bonds	2,300

The ordinary shares are trading at $2.30 and the preference shares are not traded. The bonds are currently priced at $96 per block of $100.

What is the current equity market capitalisation ($000)?

A $3,685

B $4,400

C $4,600

D $9,185

155 Jenduri is a private company that is considering listing its shares for the first time on a local stock exchange via an initial public offering (IPO). They intend to list 30% of their 4 million shares on to the market.

The company advisors have prepared the following schedule of equity valuations per share:

	$
Nominal value	0.50
Net assets – book value	2.34
Net assets – net realisable value	1.72
Dividend valuation model	3.35

What is the most appropriate valuation for the IPO?

A $0.50

B $1.72

C $2.34

D $3.35

156 Sari is a family owned company that manufactures parts to the motor industry. The entity has been struggling in recent years and the owners are now considering their options.

Extracts from the latest accounts show the book value of their assets to be worth:

	$m
Land and buildings	4.10
Plant and machinery	1.30
Inventory	0.85
Trade receivables	0.45

The company has trade payables standing at $0.66m and the bank overdraft is now at $2.15m. The non-current assets would only be worth 42% of the book values if sold immediately. Similarly, the inventory would realise $0.32m if disposed of today. A factoring company has valued the trade receivables at 72% of the book value.

The net cash available to distribute to the shareholders if the business did NOT continue as a going concern is $_____(INSERT CORRECT FIGURE IN THE BOX)

157 Zudun Co's equity is currently valued at $598m. Their last reported profit after tax was $52m. ETA Co is a family owned business that operates in the same industry as Zudun Co. ETA's board of directors is considering either a trade sale or a listing via an IPO.

Financial data relating to ETA Co:

Issued ordinary share capital ($1 shares)	3m
Profit after tax	$11.12m
Recently paid dividends	$3.34m
Estimated cost of equity	11%

ETA Co has maintained its current dividend payout ratio for the last 5 years.

Complete the following schedule relating to ETA Co:

EPS	$xx.xx
Value per share using dividend valuation model	$xx.xx
Value per share using the P/E model	$xx.xx

158 Company X is hoping to sell 100% of its 1m shares. Its current operating profit is $400,000, its profit after tax is $259,000 and a suitable PE ratio is 14.

What is the value per share for Company X?

A $2.59

B $3.63

C $3.82

D $5.60

159 **The following data applies to Abbott Co:**

Current P/E ratio = 10
Latest dividends = $2m
Dividend cover = 5

What is the market value of Abbott Co based on a P/E valuation?

A $80m

B $95m

C $100m

D $200m

160 **Clare Co is looking to value 100% of its equity.**

It currently has a profit after tax of $1.5 million, but this includes an element of profit from the sale of land of $0.325 million. A suitable P/E ratio is 8.

What is the value of Clare Co using a P/E ratio method?

A $9.4 million

B $12 million

C $15.3 million

D $18.7 million

161 **The directors of Veena Co, an unlisted entity, want to value the entity's shares using the P/E method.**

The entity recently reported a profit after tax of $800,000 – which the directors think is sustainable for the future.

They have found a similar company that is listed that has a P/E ratio of 10. From a full review it is thought that Veena Co is worth about 25% less than the listed company.

What is the value of Veena Co, using the P/E method?

A $4.3 million

B $6 million

C $8 million

D $10.4 million

162 **Company A is owned by its three directors and they want to sell the business.**

The current profit after tax is $500,000. At the moment the directors are only paid small salaries as they take most of their returns in the form of dividends.

Once the company is sold, the cost of directors' salaries in Company A will need to be increased by $40,000 in total to attract sufficiently high quality new directors.

A suitable P/E ratio is 5 and the tax rate is 30%.

What is the value of Company A, using a P/E valuation?

A $1,800,000

B $2,360,000

C $2,500,000

D $2,832,000

163 **After months of planning, Thierry Co released news to the market of its expansion strategy.**

Prior to the release, Thierry had a market capitalisation of $42.6 million, an authorised share capital of $1 million and an issued share capital of $500,000 (made up of 50 cent shares).

The expansion strategy is expected to generate an NPV of $5 million.

Assuming strong form market efficiency, what will be the effect on Thierry's share price?

A   Increase by $10

B   Increase by $5

C   No change

D   Increase by $20

164 Miss Coates has been left $20,000 which she plans to invest on the Stock Exchange in order to have a source of capital should she decide to start her own business in a few years' time. A friend of hers who works in the City of London has told her that the London Stock Exchange shows strong form market efficiency.

If this is the case, which of the following investment strategies should Miss Coates follow?

A   Study the company reports in the press and try to spot under-valued shares in which to invest

B   Invest in two or three blue chip companies and hold the shares for as long as possible

C   Build up a good spread of shares in different industry sectors

D   Study the company reports in the press and try to spot strongly growing companies in which to invest

165 Share prices quoted on a stock exchange are observed to move before information about the company's plans becomes publicly available.

Which of the following best describes this form of market efficiency?

A   Weak form

B   Strong form

C   Semi-strong form

D   Not efficient at all

166 Match the following descriptions with the types of market efficiency.

Weak form	Extrapolating past share price movements would allow a trader to beat the market.
Strong form	Accurate analysis of public information should allow a trader to beat the market.
No efficiency	All information in a market is accounted for in the share price.
Semi strong efficiency	Traders can only beat the market using insider information.

167 What is the validity of the following statements?

(1)   The existence of projects with positive expected net present values supports the idea that the stock market is strong-form efficient.

(2)   The existence of information content in dividends supports the idea that the stock market is strong-form efficient.

	Statement (1)	Statement (2)
A	True	True
B	True	False
C	False	True
D	False	False

168 Asad Co is trying to find the value of its intangible assets using the Calculated Intangible Value (CIV) method. Relevant data is:

Tangible assets	$1.268m
WACC	11%
Ke	14%
Profit before tax	$0.453m
Industry return on tangible assets	15%
Tax Rate	30%

What is the value of Asad Co's intangible assets?

A $1.672m

B $1.314m

C $1.210m

D $0.951m

169 Food2go is a supermarket with a current debt to equity ratio of 30:70 based on market values and it has a current equity beta of 0.8. To expand business it plans to take over an unlisted petrol station company, Petrol King Co, which has an estimated debt to equity ratio of 40:60.

To value Petrol King Co, Food2go intends to use the discounted cash flow approach, so it needs to calculate a suitable cost of equity as a prelude to calculating a weighted average cost of capital (WACC) that can be used for discounting.

A listed petrol station company has an equity beta of 1.8 with a debt to equity ratio of 50:50

The expected return on the market portfolio is 8% and the current return on a risk free investment is 5%. The tax rate is 30%

What cost of equity should be used as part of the WACC for discounting the Petrol King Co cash flows?

A   9.65%

B   9.50%

C   12.00%

D   5.70%

170 A portfolio is equally invested in company A, with an expected return of 6%, company B, with an expected return of 10%, and a risk-free asset with a return of 5%.

The expected return on the portfolio is:

A   6.3%

B   7.0%

C   7.4%

D   8.0%

171 Chambers has a debt : equity ratio of 1:2 by market values and an equity beta of 0.9. Debt is assumed to be risk free and has a pre-tax cost of 2% per annum. The expected return on the market portfolio is 8% and corporation tax is 30%.

Chambers wishes to undertake an APV approach for investment appraisal.

What is the ungeared cost of equity for Chambers to use in such an evaluation?

- A 6.00%
- B 7.40%
- C 9.20%
- D 9.29%

172 Clyne has a debt : equity ratio of 1:2 by market values and an asset beta of 0.9. Debt is assumed to be risk free and has a pre-tax cost of 2% per annum. The market risk premium is 8% and corporation tax is 30%.

What is Clyne's geared cost of equity?

- A 7.40%
- B 9.20%
- C 9.29%
- D 11.72%

173 Fonte has a debt : equity ratio of 1:2 by market values and an equity beta of 0.9. Debt is assumed to be risk free and has a pre-tax cost of 2% per annum. The market risk premium is 8% and corporation tax is 30%.

What is Fonte's geared cost of equity?

- A 7.40%
- B 9.20%
- C 9.29%
- D 11.72%

174 Lovren has a debt : equity ratio of 1:2 by market values and an asset beta of 0.9. Debt is assumed to be risk free and has a pre-tax cost of 2% per annum. The expected return on the market portfolio is 8% and corporation tax is 30%.

What is Lovren's geared cost of equity?

- A 7.40%
- B 9.20%
- C 9.29%
- D 11.72%

175 Shaw has a debt : equity ratio of 1:2 by market values and an equity beta of 0.9. Debt is assumed to be risk free and has a pre-tax cost of 2% per annum. The expected return on the market portfolio is 8% and corporation tax is 30%.

What is Shaw's geared cost of equity?

A   7.40%

B   9.20%

C   9.29%

D   11.72%

176 **You have been asked to calculate the equity beta factor for SIX Co.**

Introductory data:

APPLE Co is a listed company in the same industry as SIX Co. It has an equity beta of 1.45.

Gearing levels – (debt/equity) by market value:

SIX Co   45/55

APPLE Co   30/70

Tax rate is 20%. The beta of debt is 0.10.

Which one of the following shows the correct formula for REGEARING the proxy company's ASSET beta (which would be the second step in trying to calculate an equity beta for SIX Co):

A $\beta_g = 1.25 + \left[(1.25 - 0.10)\left(\dfrac{30(1 - 0.25)}{70} \right) \right]$

B $\beta_g = 1.12 + \left[(1.12 - 0.10)\left(\dfrac{30(1 - 0.25)}{70} \right) \right]$

C $\beta_g = 1.12 + \left[(1.12 - 0.10)\left(\dfrac{45(1 - 0.25)}{55} \right) \right]$

D $\beta_g = 1.25 + \left[(1.25 - 0.10)\left(\dfrac{45(1 - 0.25)}{55} \right) \right]$

177 Ocatvio Co is preparing a valuation of Tarte Co, an unlisted company. Tarte Co has an estimated debt to equity ratio of 20% : 80%.

As part of the calculation of a suitable weighted average cost of capital, Octavio Co needs to identify a suitable equity beta for Tarte Co.

The following information has been presented by Octavio Co's Financial Controller, based on three other companies that share the same business risk as Tarte Co, but have different capital structures.

Co A   Equity beta = 1.6   Debt to equity ratio 40:60

Co B   Equity beta = 1.2   Debt to equity ratio 10:90

Co C   Equity beta = 1.8   Debt to equity ratio 50:50

Which of the following is the best estimate of the correct equity beta for Tarte Co?

A   1.0

B   1.4

C   1.7

D   2.0

178 Turtle Power Co is an unlisted company. Its directors are preparing a valuation of the company that will be used in negotiations with a potential purchaser. Hence they need to compute a suitable weighted average cost of capital.

The entity currently has an estimated debt to equity ratio of 15:85. Its debt is approximately risk free and has a pre-tax cost of 4%.

A similar quoted company to Turtle Power Co has an equity beta of 1.2, and a debt to equity ratio of 30:70.

The expected return on the market portfolio is 10% and the tax rate is 30%.

What is the weighted average cost of capital of Turtle Power Co?

A   9.1%

B   9.3%

C   9.9%

D   10.1%

179 Forrest Co has a debt to equity ratio of 30:70 and has an equity beta of 1.4. The tax rate is 30%.

The current return on a risk free asset is 5% and the average market risk premium is 7%.

What is Forrest Co's ungeared cost of equity?

A   5.9%

B   12.6%

C   14.1%

D   20.5%

180 **Exercise Co is attempting to derive its cost of equity, based on the following proxy company information: a similar company in the same industry has an equity beta of 1.6 with a debt to equity ratio of 20:80.**

Exercise Co has an estimated debt to equity ratio of 30:70.

The expected return on the market portfolio is 8% and the current return on a risk free investment is 4%. The tax rate is 30%

What is Exercise Co's cost of equity?

A   15.0%

B   9.8%

C   11.1%

D   27.6%

181 **QPR is a listed company which is seeking to sell WBA, one of its business units, in a management buyout. A selling price of $100 million has been agreed. It is anticipated that the date of the disposal will be 1 January 20X5.**

The managers of WBA have been in discussions with a bank and a venture capitalist regarding the financing for the MBO. The financing proposal is:

	$m
Managers – equity	25
VC – equity	15
VC – debt	40
Bank loan	20
Total	100

The venture capitalist expects a return on the equity portion of its investment of at least 20% a year on a compound basis over the first 3 years of the MBO.

What is the minimum total equity value of WBA on 31 December 20X8 required in order to satisfy the venture capitalist's expected return?

A $69.12 million

B $25.92 million

C $18.00 million

D $48.00 million

182 **Willis incorporated a new company five years ago. The company has grown quickly and is now large enough to be listed on the stock exchange. Willis owns 100% of the share capital in the company and wishes to realise the full value of his investment.**

Which THREE of the following exit strategies could Willis consider?

A   Rights issue of shares

B   Spin off

C   Management buy-out

D   Initial public offering (IPO)

E   Private equity buy-in

183 **Company A wishes to acquire company B and is considering how best to structure the consideration. Both companies are of a similar size.**

A currently has gearing (D/D+E) of 40%. A's shareholders do not wish to subscribe additional funds at this time.

Structuring the bid offer as a cash offer funded by debt rather than a share exchange is MOST likely to have the effect of:

A   Diluting A shareholders' control

B   Increasing A shareholders' earnings per share

C   Lowering A's gearing (D/D+E)

D   Enabling B's shareholders to participate in future growth in A

184 **Two all-equity financed companies, Spain Co and France Co, have identical business risks. Spain Co is valued at $30 million and France Co at $10 million.**

The two companies merge via a share exchange which results in Spain Co shareholders holding 75% of the shares of the new merged company.

As a result of synergy, surplus assets of $6 million are sold immediately without affecting the future profitability of the merged company. Half of the proceeds of the disposal are invested in a project with a net present value of $2 million.

What will be the gains to the shareholders of France Co?

A $6.00 million

B $3.75 million

C $1.25 million

D $2.00 million

185 **GGG Co takes over FFF Co and pays a price that represents a higher P/E valuation than the current P/E of GGG Co.**

GGG Co has some debt in its capital structure, and the purchase consideration is paid by issuing new GGG Co shares. There is no synergy arising from the takeover.

Which of the following would NOT be a likely consequence of this takeover?

A   a reduction in gearing for GGG Co

B   an increase in the share price after the takeover

C   a reduction in the proportionate stake in the company of existing GGG Co shareholders

D   a dilution of earnings of GGG Co

186 **Stone Co is hoping to make a successful takeover offer for Angel Co.**

Stone Co is a large listed company, with a wide range of both institutional and private shareholders.

It has relatively low cash reserves and a gearing ratio of 40% that is higher than most similar companies in its industry.

Which TWO of the following would be feasible ways of structuring an offer for Angel Co?

A   Cash offer, funded by borrowings

B   Share for share exchange

C   Cash offer, funded from existing cash resources

D   Cash offer, funded by a rights issue

E   Debt for share exchange

187 **SS has proposed a 1-for-3 share for share exchange with the shareholders of TT, so that SS can acquire TT.**

The two companies operate in the same industry and it is estimated that synergy with a present value of $2 million will be generated by the combination.

Currently, SS has 12 million shares in issue, trading at $6.76, and TT has 3 million shares in issue trading at $1.97.

What is the expected share price in the combined company after the takeover?

A $6.85

B $6.76

C $5.91

D $3.17

188 Udika Co has agreed buy all the share capital of Tito Co. The board of directors of Udika Co believes that the post-acquisition value of their business including Tito can be computed using the "bootstrapping" method.

This can be found by:

A   Combining the pre-acquisition market capitalisation of each company

B   Adding together the current post tax earnings of each company and multiplying this by the price earnings ratio of Tito

C   Adding together the current post tax earnings of each company and multiplying this by the price earnings ratio of Udika

D   Forecasting the future free cash flows of the combined entities and discounting these at Udika's WACC

189 Which of the following best describes an earn-out?

A   an arrangement where the owners/managers selling an entity receive a portion of their consideration linked to the financial performance of the business

B   a situation where an entity is valued using the price-earnings ratio

C   a method of splitting the profits of an entity between its various financial stakeholders

D   a situation where an entity generates more than a quarter of its earnings from activities different from its main line of business

190 Oban Co has agreed the purchase of all of the share capital of Reeves Inc. Relevant financial details are:

Reeves EPS	$0.34
Oban profit after tax	$25.2m
Oban – number of issued shares	126m
Oban – current share price	$4.00
Reeves – current share price	$4.25
Reeves – number of shares in issue	20m

If Oban can maintain its current P/E ratio, what is the value of the synergy gained from acquiring Reeves?

A $51m

B $85m

C $145m

D $563m

191 **Fitness Co is an unlisted company, which was incorporated five years ago and is still 90% owned by its founding family.**

The managers are planning to embark upon a period of expansion by acquisition, but the company has very little cash. Therefore, a share for share exchange is being considered in order for Fitness Co to acquire Dumbell Co, a similar sized company in the same industry whose shareholders are keen to realise cash from their investment.

Which of the following problems is LEAST likely to be an issue in this situation?

A   Fitness Co's founding family will suffer a significant dilution in control

B   Dumbell Co's shareholders will find it difficult to evaluate the bid given that Fitness Co is unlisted

C   Fitness Co has very little cash, so won't be able to afford to take over Dumbell Co

D   Dumbell Co's shareholders will not receive the cash that they require in a share for share exchange

192 **MMM is intending to make a bid for JJJ.**

MMM has 30 million shares in issue and a current share price of $6.90 before any public announcement of the planned takeover.

JJJ has 5 million shares in issue and a current share price of $12.84.

The directors of MMM are considering making a share based bid of 2 MMM shares for each JJJ share. Overall estimated synergistic benefits of the acquisition are estimated to be in the order of $8 million.

What is the likely gain in wealth for the MMM shareholders if the bid is accepted?

A $2.40 million

B $5.60 million

C $6.98 million

D $8.00 million

193 **AB has recently approached the shareholders of YZ with a bid of 5 new shares in AB for every 6 YZ shares. There is a cash alternative of 345 cents per share.**

Following the announcement of the bid, the market price of AB shares fell 10% while the price of YZ shares rose 14%.

Enter the correct word from the choices given:

The market believes that the shareholders of _____(AB/YZ) will receive most of the benefit from this acquisition.

This could be because the value of the offer is too _____(high/low).

194 **Enter the correct word from the choices given, to create two statements that apply to a share for share exchange:**

Compared to a cash offer, a share for share exchange is _____(more/less) likely to create a liability to capital gains tax.

A share for share exchange will benefit the target company's shareholders more than a cash offer if the combined entity performs _____(well/badly) after the acquisition.

195 **The directors of Q have approached the directors of Z with a view to making a takeover bid for Z, an owner-managed business.**

The directors of Q want to retain the board of directors of Z, who have vital knowledge of the specialist manufacturing techniques required to manufacture the product range of Z.

The directors of Z have been initially quite positive about the bid.

Which of the following types of offer would be MOST suitable in these circumstances?

A   Cash offer

B   Share for share exchange

C   Earnout

D   Debt for share exchange

196 **LP and MQ are two listed companies.**

LP made an opening bid one week ago of 2 LP shares for 1 MQ share, but MQ's shareholders have rejected the bid.

	LP	MQ
Share price as at today (20 May 20X9)	$3.05	$6.80
Share price one month ago	$3.10	$6.10
Shares in issue (million)	480	130

Which of the following bids would the MQ shareholders be MOST likely to accept?

A   1.97 LP shares for 1 MQ share

B   2.23 LP shares for 1 MQ share

C   2.5 LP shares for 1 MQ share

D   3 LP shares for 1 MQ share

197 **Astor Co is planning to acquire Baker Co.**

Astor Co currently has post tax earnings of $23.5 million and a P/E ratio of 9. Baker Co currently has post tax earnings of $9.5 million and a P/E ratio of 7.

What is the value of the synergy that will be generated by the combination of Astor Co and Baker Co, assuming that the market uses bootstrapping to calculate the value of the combined entity?

A   Nil

B $19.0 million

C $66.5 million

D $278.0 million

198 Glenderaterra Co and Mungrisdale Co are planning to merge using a share for share exchange. Glenderaterra Co has offered one of its shares for every three shares in Mungrisdale Co.

The directors expect that $10 million of synergy will be generated by combining the two entities.

Current market information shows:

	Glenderaterra	Mungrisdale
Share price	$3.88	$1.10
Shares in issue (million)	50	12

What share of the synergy gain will accrue to the shareholders of Mungrisdale?

A   None

B   29%

C   71%

D   91%

199 Orc Co is considering a takeover bid for Sauron Co.

In which of the following circumstances is a debt for share exchange likely to be MOST suitable?

A   Sauron Co's shareholders are keen to realise cash for their investment

B   Orc Co has a gearing level higher than the average for companies in its industry

C   Sauron Co's shareholders want to maintain an interest in the combined company, but the Orc Co shareholders do not want to suffer a dilution of control

D   Sauron Co is a small company, and its shareholders are the same people as its lenders

200 MMM is intending to make a bid for JJJ.

MMM has 30 million shares in issue and a current share price of $6.90 before any public announcement of the planned takeover.

JJJ has 5 million shares in issue and a current share price of $12.84.

The directors of MMM are considering making a cash offer of $13.50 per JJJ share. Overall estimated synergistic benefits of the acquisition are estimated to be in the order of $8 million.

What is the likely change in wealth for the MMM shareholders if the bid is accepted?

A   Loss of $59.50 million

B   No change

C   Gain of $4.70 million

D   Gain of $8.00 million

Section 2

ANSWERS TO OBJECTIVE TEST QUESTIONS

SYLLABUS SECTION A: FORMULATION OF FINANCIAL STRATEGY

1   A

Creditors bear the responsibility for bankruptcy in that they will not receive the principal back from their investment. If the project is a great success, creditors' returns will not increase; they will only receive the money loaned plus interest. On the other hand, shareholders could see the value of their shares rise many times over, while the reputation of the managers (and their bonuses) is likely to rapidly increase.

2   A

Although the over-riding objective of every listed company is to maximise shareholder wealth, the specific financial objectives listed in a company's annual report would not normally make reference to this.

The gearing objective is too vague B because gearing can be measured in several different ways (e.g. debt to equity or debt to (debt + equity) and at book value or at market value).

The expansion objective should contain numbers so that its achievement can be measured C – all objectives should be measurable.

The dividend growth objective should be linked to company performance D or there is a danger that earnings growth might not keep up with dividend growth, causing financial difficulties.

3   A, D

Both for-profit and not-for-profit entities aim to satisfy a wide range of stakeholders B.

Not-for-profit entities don't have profit oriented objectives but they may well have financial objectives C.

4   D

Managers succeed in acting without due regard to the interests of shareholders when they have access to better information about the business than shareholders and when they are insufficiently accountable for their decisions and actions.

5   A

When the entity was privatised, it changed from being a public sector to a private sector entity. The fact that its shares are traded on the stock market and that it operates in a competitive market place suggests that it is a for-profit entity.

6   A

Market value of debt is $800,000 × (94/100) = $752,000

Market value of equity = 1 million × $1.47 = $1,470,000

Therefore, gearing is [752/1,470] = 51.2%

7   D

The annual return to investors is:

$[(P_1 - P_0) + \text{Dividend}]/ P_0$

where P_0 is $6.10, P_1 is $6.45 and Dividend is $0.30.

8   B

9   B, C

Earnings yield is the reciprocal of P/E ratio, so a high P/E will correspond to a low earnings yield.

A high P/E ratio shows that investors have confidence in the company.

10   C

Dividend pay-out ratio is (dividend per share/earnings per share), dividend yield is (dividend per share/share price) and P/E ratio is (share price/earnings per share).

Therefore, P/E ratio = (dividend pay-out ratio/dividend yield) = 0.20/0.08 = 2.5

11   B

ROCE can be found by multiplying asset turnover and operating profit margin.

12   A

13   B

Gross profit margin = ($1,000 sales − $600 COGS)/$1,000 sales

= 400/1,000

= 0.4 or 40%

Operating profit margin = ($1,000 sales − $600 COGS − $200 op expenses)/$1,000 sales

= $200/$1,000

= 0.2 or 20%

14   C

Operating profit/interest = 100,000 /25,000 =4

15   C

The higher the percentage of an entity's expenses that are fixed, the higher the operating leverage, and the greater the entity's business risk and the more susceptible it is to business cycle fluctuations.

16   A

When the US dollar depreciates, the opposing currency appreciates (inverse relationship). The depreciation of the dollar means that foreign goods become more expensive and import prices will increase. Conversely, as the value of the dollar decreases, US goods become cheaper to foreign customers and US export prices will decrease.

17   C

A currency appreciates when it rises in value relative to another foreign currency. Likewise, a currency depreciates when it falls in value relative to another foreign currency. An appreciation in value of a currency makes that country's goods more expensive to residents of other countries. The depreciation of the value of a currency makes a country's goods more attractive to foreign buyers.

18   C

$[\sqrt[5]{(2.9/2.2)}] - 1 = 5.7\%$

19   D

Dividend per share has grown from $12 (120/10) to $13.08 (170/13).

Therefore the annual growth in dividend per share is:

$[\sqrt[4]{(13.08/12)}] - 1 = 2.2\%$

20   A

$[\sqrt[4]{(0.28/0.20)}] - 1 = 8.8\%$

21   A

The H$ is the base currency and the EUR is the variable, so the forward rate is

$6.250 \times (1.02/1.06) = 6.014$

22   C

The GBP is the base currency and the EUR is the variable, so the forward rate is

$1.2400 \times (1.0075/1.005) = 1.2431$

23   B

$1.2075 \times (1.02)^2 = 1.2563$

24   D

The W$ is the base currency and the EUR is the variable, so the future expected rate is

$1.9900 \times (1.01/1.08) = 1.8610$

Therefore, the value of the transaction is EUR 100,000/1.8610 = W$ 53,735

25   C

The C$ is the base currency and the USD is the variable, so the future expected rate is

$1.1144 \times (1.03/1.05)^{0.5} = 1.1037$

26   B, D, E

The other two sections should appear in the social category of the specific standard disclosures, not the general standard disclosures.

27   A, B, E

C is an objective of sustainability reporting.

D is irrelevant – investors are more interested in the quality, not the quantity, of information available.

28   A, D, E

The other two are Principles for Defining Report Quality according to the GRI.

29   B

In exceptional cases, if it is not possible to disclose certain required information, the report should clearly identify the information that has been omitted, and explain the reasons why the information has been omitted.

30   B

Social and relationship capitals include intangibles associated with the brand and reputation that an organisation has developed.

31   D

32   A, C, F

C and F are simply the wrong way round i.e. Risks and opportunities is really a content element and Consistency and comparability is a guiding principle.

A should not appear in an Integrated Report. However it would appear as a specific standard disclosure in a sustainability report prepared using the GRI Guidelines.

33   B, D

Paying a large dividend to shareholders A will make no difference to the wealth of shareholders. Raising new equity finance C in an all-equity financed entity will not affect the cost of capital and will not affect shareholder wealth (unless the finance raised is invested in a positive NPV project).

A positive NPV project increases shareholder wealth B.

If an all-equity financed company raises debt finance D its cost of capital will fall, giving an increase in the NPVs generated from projects and hence an increase in shareholder wealth.

34   D

Regulators generally try to ensure that decisions are not just made with the interests of shareholders in mind, but that other important factors are considered.

35   Thursday Co will probably find it **easier** to raise debt finance than Cass Co.

The rate of interest on borrowings is likely to be **lower** for Thursday Co than Cass Co.

36   Holding **too little** cash will potentially leave the entity subject to liquidity problems and possible liquidation.

Holding **too much** cash has an opportunity cost (lost interest on deposits, or returns on attractive investments).

Holding **too much** cash leaves an entity vulnerable to a takeover bid.

37   D

To earn maximum returns on investment assets is not a valid reason for a business to hold cash and marketable securities. Note: Non-current assets generally have a greater return than current assets, particularly cash.

38   B

	With 100% equity	With 60% equity
EBIT	$300,000	$300,000
Interest expense	$0	$24,000 ($480,000 @ 5%)
Profit before tax	$300,000	$276,000
Tax @ 30%	$90,000	$82,800
Net profit	$210,000	$193,200
Equity	$1,200,000	$720,000
ROE = Net profit/Equity	17.5%	26.8%

39   D

Dividend growth:

From $0.55m to $0.70m amounts to approximately 27.3% growth in total

(= [0.70/0.55] − 1).

Over three years, the annual growth is found by taking [$\sqrt[3]{1.273}$] − 1 = 8.4%, so above the target of 7% − objective achieved

Gearing:

Debt value is $105 × 10,000 = $1.05 million

Equity value is 2 million × $1.24 = $2.48 million

So [debt/(debt + equity)] = [1.05/(1.05 + 2.48)] = 29.7%, so below the target of 30% − objective achieved

40   B

Interest cover will be

[25m/(6% × 60m) + (5% × 40m)] = 4.46, which is above the level set by the covenant so the covenant is not breached.

41   B

Revenue will be 1.50 million × 1.04 = USD 1.56 million this year i.e. GBP 0.945 million

(1.56/1.6500)

Assume cost of sales will stay constant (since sales volume stays constant) at GBP 0.67 million.

Then, gross profit margin will be [(0.945 − 0.67)/0.945] = 29.1%

42   D

C is under normal accounting rules.

A and B are incorrect.

43   A

According to IAS 39 gains and losses on designated hedging instruments (the loan) and hedged items (the net investment in Wine Co) are recorded in other comprehensive income. Any gain or loss on the unhedged element of the investment (the GBP 200,000 not covered by the loan) is recognised in the statement of profit or loss.

44   B, C, E

Conditions for hedge accounting to be permitted are:

- There is formal designation and documentation of the hedging relationship at the inception of the hedge.
- The hedge is expected to be highly effective.
- The effectiveness of the hedge can be reliably measured.
- The hedge is assessed on an ongoing basis and has actually been highly effective throughout the financial reporting periods for which it was designated.
- (Cash flow hedges only) The forecast transaction that is the subject of the hedge must be highly probable and must present an exposure to variations in cash flows that could ultimately affect profit or loss.

45   B

Stock brokers use financial instruments for trading purposes (speculation) and should use normal accounting rules.

All the other businesses are more likely to use a financial instrument for hedging purposes and should use the hedge accounting rules.

46   D

This transaction is a cash flow hedge. Because the forward contract has no fair value at its inception, the need to account for the derivative first arises at the end of the reporting period when it has a value and the change in value has to be recorded. Because it has been designated a cash flow hedge, the change in value is recognised in other comprehensive income to be carried forward at 31 July to match against the future cash flow. The value of this contract is in showing a loss of EUR 10,000 at the end of the reporting period because LINE Co is locked into buying USD 200,000 for EUR 200,000 when everyone else can buy for EUR 190,000, hence LINE Co is EUR 10,000 worse off because it hedged the position.

To recognise the loss:

Dr Other comprehensive income EUR 10,000

Cr Liability – derivative EUR 10,000

Note that if this transaction had not been designated a hedging instrument then the loss would be recognised immediately in profit or loss.

47   A

Both the investment and the loan will initially be translated at historic rate and retranslated at closing rate at the year end:

Investment			Loan		
Historic rate	EUR 500m/0.81	USD 617.3m	Historic rate	EUR 430m/0.81	USD 530.9m
Closing rate	EUR 500m/0.79	USD 632.9m	Closing rate	EUR 430m/0.79	USD 544.3m
	GAIN	USD 15.6m		LOSS	USD 13.4m

The gain and loss is offset against each other in OCI, and the hedge would be considered 86% (13.4/15.6) effective.

48   A

D relates to normal accounting rules rather than hedge accounting rules.

B is wrong – the copper value has increased, not decreased.

C is wrong for a fair value hedge.

49   C

IFRS 9 will replace IAS 39 on 1 January 2018.

50   A

Forward contracts are custom-tailored contracts and are not exchange traded while futures contracts are standardised and are traded on an organised exchange.

SYLLABUS SECTION B: FINANCING AND DIVIDEND DECISIONS

51   C

If gearing is very low, then there is scope for the company to raise finance by means of cheap debt.

If interest rates are rising or there was an expected loss that would be a disincentive to raise more debt.

52   A

Buying treasury bills and paying cash dividends will decrease shareholders' equity, and thus increase the debt/equity ratio. Converting long-term debt to short-term will have no effect on total debt or shareholders' equity. Lowering dividend payout ratio will increase retained earnings, thus increasing shareholders' equity and decreasing debt/equity ratio.

53   B

An entity's target or optimal capital structure is not consistent with minimum risk A because the optimum capital structure minimises cost, not risk.

An entity's target or optimal capital structure is not consistent with maximum earnings per share C. An entity's target or optimal capital structure minimises the cost of capital, not the overall maximum earnings per share.

An entity's target or optimal capital structure is not consistent with minimum cost of debt D. An entity's target or optimal capital structure is concerned with minimising the cost of debt and equity, not just debt.

54   C

An entity's capital structure affects both its return on equity and its risk of default. More equity would reduce the return on equity and more debt would increase the risk of default.

55   A

An increase in the corporate income tax rate might cause an entity to increase the debt in its capital structure.

Increased economic uncertainty B would not cause an entity to increase the debt in its capital structure.

An increase in the base rate of interest C would not cause an entity to increase the debt in its capital structure.

An increase in the price/earnings ratio D would not cause an entity to increase the debt in its capital structure.

56   B, C, F

The key assumptions of Modigliani and Miller's 1963 gearing theory are:

- Companies do pay tax
- The capital market is strongly efficient
- There are no transaction costs
- Debt is risk free
- Cost of debt stays constant at all levels of gearing
- Investors are indifferent between personal and corporate gearing
- Investors and companies can borrow at the same rate of interest

So the correct three points were the second, third and sixth on the list (i.e. companies do pay tax, there are no transaction costs and cost of debt stays constant at all levels of gearing)

57   B

Modigliani and Miller's 1963 gearing theory is the 'with tax' theory. It concludes that the cost of capital reduces as the gearing level increases.

58   D

The traditional view of gearing concludes that the cost of capital follows a U shaped curve, and therefore that there is an optimum gearing level at which the cost of capital is minimised and the value of the company is maximised.

59   A

Modigliani and Miller's formula is:

$$k_{adj} = k_{eu} \times [1 - (tL)]$$

where L is (D/(D+E))

Therefore, the correct answer is the first one on the list.

60   B

Modigliani and Miller's formula is:

$$k_{eg} = k_{eu} + [(k_{eu} - k_d) \times \left(V_D(1-t) \Big/ V_E \right)]$$

where k_d is the yield to the debt holders.

Therefore, the correct answer is the second one on the list.

61   C

Modigliani and Miller's formula is:

$$V_g = V_u + TD$$

Therefore, the value of the company if it funds the project using the bond is Vu (the value if the company continued to be all equity financed) plus 20% × $20 million (i.e. $4 million).

Vu can be found by discounting the earnings figure as a perpetuity.

So

$$V_u = \frac{30m}{0.15} = \$200m$$

Therefore, Vg = $200 million + $4 million = $204 million.

Finally, if the value of the company is $204 million, but this incorporates $20 million of debt, the equity value must be $184 million, the third answer on the list.

62   C

Interest is paid regardless of the performance of the company, providing a more predictable return for investors, lowering the risk of investment.

Tax deductibility is not relevant here, as M&M's 1958 model assumes no corporation tax.

63   C

Vg = Vu + TB

= $72m + ($36.2m*0.33) = $83.946m

Less debt $36.2m = $47.746m

Divide by 10m shares = $4.77

A Forgot to divide by number of shares

B No tax effect

D Same as Co C

64   A

Keg = 17.5% + (17.5%–7.5%) × [1(1–0.33)/2] = 20.85%

65   C

The return to shareholders becomes less variable when gearing is lower.

66   A

As gearing increases WACC first falls due to the lower cost of debt, but as k_e begins to increase rapidly, this dominates and WACC rises.

67   The answer is 8.8%

$K_{adj} = K_{eu} (1\text{-}tL)$

$0.094 = K_{eu} (1 - 0.3 \times 0.2)$

$0.094 = K_{eu} \times 0.94$

$K_{eu} = 0.1$

$K_{adj} = 0.1 \times (1 - 0.3 \times 0.4)$

WACC = 0.088 = 8.8%

68   D

$V_g = V_u + TB$

$V_g = 60 + 0.3 \times 20$

$V_g = 66$

$K_{adj} = K_{eu}(1\text{-}tL)$

$K_{adj} = 0.15 (1 - 0.3 \times 20/66)$

$K_{adj} = 0.136 = 13.6\%$

69   The answer is 22.22%

$K_{eu} = 15\%$ (current WACC)

Required WACC = 14%

$K_{adj} = K_{eu} (1\text{-}tL)$

$0.14 = 0.15 (1 - 0.3xL)$

$0.14 = 0.15 - 0.045L$

$0.045L = 0.01$

$L = 0.2222$

70 The answer is **6.4%**

$K_{adj} = K_{eu} (1-tL)$

$0.094 = K_{eu} (1- 0.3 \times 0.2)$

$0.094 = 0.94 \times K_{eu}$

$K_{eu} = 0.1$

$K_{adj} = 0.1 \times (1 - 0.3 \times 0.4)$

WACC = 0.088

% change =(9.4 − 8.8)/9.4

71 The answer is **13.42%**

$K_{eg} = K_{eu} + (K_{eu} − K_d) \times D(1-t)/E$

$0.14 = K_{eu} + (K_{eu} − 0.08) \times 8 \times 0.7/52$

$0.14 = K_{eu} + 0.1077(K_{eu} − 0.08)$

$0.14 = K_{eu} + 0.1077K_{eu} − 0.008616$

$0.1486 = 1.1077K_{eu}$

$0.1486/1.1077 = K_{eu} = 0.1342 = WACC$

Note: WACC = K_{eu} for an ungeared company

72 **The answer is:**

	Insert letter
Wealth maximising capital structure	C
Conservative capital structure	A
Aggressive capital structure	B
Theoretical capital structure	D

Point D, full gearing, is theoretical only. Covenants in existing debt and an unwillingness to lend to excessively geared companies would prevent this from being achieved in practice.

73 **B**

74 **D**

M&M argue that because of the tax advantage of debt, the higher the gearing, the lower the WACC and the higher the market value of the entity.

75 The answer is **14.4%**

$WACC = k_{eu}(1 − tL)$

Where L = Debt/(Debt + Equity) = 1/5 = 0.2

So WACC = 0.15[1 − (0.2)(0.2)] = 0.144 (14.4%)

76 The answer is **14.7%**

$k_{eg} = k_{eu} + (k_{eu} - K_d)(V_d/V_e)(1 - t)$

$0.14 = k_{eu} + (k_{eu} - 0.08)(0.4)(0.8)$

$0.14 = k_{eu} + (k_{eu} - 0.08)(0.32)$

$0.14 = k_{eu} + 0.32k_{eu} - 0.0256$

$1.32k_{eu} = 0.1656$

$k_{eu} = 0.12545$

Then, with new gearing level:

$k_{eg} = 0.12545 + (0.12545 - 0.08)(0.6)(0.8)$

$\quad = 0.14727$

Therefore: 14.7%

77 The answer is **$10.01**

		$m
$V_u = 10m \times 9.50$	=	95
$V_g = V_u + TB$		
$V_g = 95 + 0.2(20)$	=	99
Less : Value of debt	=	(20)
V_e	=	79

No. shares repurchased (20m/9.5)	=	2,105,263.16
No. shares remaining (10m – 20m/9.5)	=	7,894,736.84
Value per share (79m/7,894,736.84)	=	10.0067
	Therefore	**$10.01**

78 C

Bonds and shares are traded on both the Primary and Secondary markets.

79 D

Interest rate risk is the probability of an increase in interest rates causing a bond's price to decrease.

80 D

Interest is tax deductible; therefore, the firm's cost of debt would be the percentage cost of the bonds less the tax effect.

81   D

Interest is tax deductible; therefore, the firm's cost of debt is cheaper than its cost of equity and its cost of preference shares.

Mezzanine debt is high risk debt finance, so tends to carry a higher interest rate than bonds.

82   The interest cover ratio must be higher than 3

The ratio of net debt to EBITDA must be lower than 3

An entity is perceived to be risky if its interest cover ratio is low and/or its net debt to EBITDA ratio is high.

83   A

The rest would increase gearing even further.

84   D

$28 \times 3.20 \times 1.03^4 = \$100.85$ which makes the shares worth more than the $100 cash. Of course this is dependent on the predicted growth of 3% per annum being achieved.

Note: By trial and error:

$28 \times 3.20 = 89.60$

$89.6 \times 1.03 = 92.29$

$89.6 \times 1.03^2 = 95.06$

$89.6 \times 1.03^3 = 97.91$

$89.6 \times 1.03^4 = 100.85$ This is more than $100 and makes the conversion worthwhile

85   A

The rest of the statements are true.

86   D

All the other answers relate to finance leases.

87   B

If leasing the relevant cash flows are the lease payments and the tax relief on these lease payments. As the lease payment is in advance, it will run from year 0 – 3 and the tax relief is one year in arrears, so will run from 2 – 5. The discount rate is 6%, being the post-tax cost of borrowing ($8.57\% \times (1-0.30)$).

Therefore, PV = $[- \$275,000 \times (1+2.673)] + [\$82,500 \times (4.212 - 0.943)] = - \$740,000$

88   C

The asset costs $450,000. The total lease payments are $120,000 × 4 = $480,000, therefore interest charged is $30,000. Using the sum of the digits method, we have 4 × 5/2 = 10 (or for a 4 year period 4 + 3 + 2 + 1 = 10)

Year	interest	tax relief @30%
1	4/10 × 30,000 = 12,000	3,600
2	3/10 × 30,000 = 9,000	2,700
3	2/10 × 30,000 = 6,000	1,800
4	1/10 × 30,000 = 3,000	900

89 $370,000

Discount rate is post-tax cost of borrowing = 7.14% × (1 − 0.30) = 5%

Year	Cashflow	5% DR	PV
0	(500)	1	(500)
1-5	(500/5) × 30%	4.329	130
NPV			(370)

90   B

It is assumed that leasing is a substitute for borrowing and so a rate that represents the risk involved should be used. As the lessee can receive tax relief on interest, the post-tax cost of borrowing is appropriate.

91   D

There is a bigger difference in the variable rates so to take advantage of this, B will borrow variable and A then has to borrow at a fixed rate. Use L% to get B on fixed and A on variable. Then 3.5% is the balancing figure to split the saving on an equal basis.

It would work out like:

	Co A	Co B
Paid to bank	(7%)	(L+2%)
A pays B	(L)	L
B pays A	3.5%	(3.5%)
Net effect	(L+3.5%)	(5.5%)

92   A, B, D

Interest rate swaps can be used to protect the fair value of fixed rate debt instruments, not floating rate debt instruments.

93   C

DD Co pays LIBOR + 1.5% at the moment and the bank has offered a swap at the rate of 5% for LIBOR (i.e. DD Co will pay 5% to the bank in exchange for LIBOR).

Hence the net rate is (LIBOR + 1.5%) +5% − LIBOR = 6.5%

94   C

An investment bank would be able to organise all aspects of an IPO (including underwriting if necessary). A stockbroker would usually only deal with smaller issues and placings.

95   D

$$\frac{5\times\$5+1\times £3.50}{5+1}=\$4.75$$

96   A

A 1 for 3 rights issues will mean 5 million new shares will be issued. This will mean there will be 20 million shares in total after the rights issue.

If the TERP is $4.80, the total value of the company after the rights issue will be 20 million × $4.80 = $96 million

The value of the company cum-rights was 15 million × $5 = $75 million.

The value of finance raised must therefore be $96 million – $75 million = $21 million.

97   D

The cum rights price is the share price before the rights issue. The issue price is normally below the current market price to give the shareholders an incentive to take up their rights. This results in an ex rights price which falls between the original market price and the issue price, calculated as a weighted average.

98   B

With a 10% market discount, the issue price would = $3 × 0.9 = $2.70

$$\frac{\$3\times5+\$2.70\times2}{7}=\$2.91$$

99   C

Answer A is a potential correct answer although it isn't necessary to offer a discount for this reason. Answer D would only be relevant if a rights issue was not successful and was followed by a new issue of shares.

If the market price of a share was to fall in the offer period, there is a risk that the rights issue will fail, as it would be cheaper to buy more shares in the market than it would to take up the offer under the rights issue. This is therefore the main reason why a discount would be offered.

100   D

If all the gain goes to existing shareholders, the market value of their shares will rise.

The new shares will have the same market value.

As there is no gain available for the new shareholders, they must have paid this (higher) market value for their shares.

101 The answer is **$1,500,000**

Current total MV (10m @$5)	50,000,000
Add: NPV	1,885,000
New funds raised	5,280,000
New total MV ($)	57,165,000
Existing number of shares	10,000,000
Add: New shares issued (5.28m/4.80)	1,100,000
New number of shares	11,100,000

MV per share	$5.15
Existing MV/cost	($5.00)
Gain per share	$0.15
Total gain	$1,500,000

102 **18.03%**

Current total MV	50,000,000
Add: NPV	2,440,000
New funds	5,280,000
New total MV	57,720,000
Existing number of shares	10,000,000
Add: New shares issued (5.28m/4.80)	1,100,000
New number of shares	11,100,000

	Shareholders		
	Existing	*New*	*Total*
MV per share	5.20	5.20	
Existing MV/cost	(5.00)	(4.80)	
Gain per share	0.20	0.40	
Total gain	2,000,000	440,000	2,440,000
Percentage	81.97%	18.03%	

103 $2.60

	$m
Current total MV (30m shares @ $2.50)	75
Add: Gain accruing to existing shareholders (=NPV)	3
New value of existing shares	78
=> Value per share (78m/30m)	**$2.60**

Since there is no gain available for the new investor, this must be the price he pays for his shares

104 The answer is **$0.39**

Current total MV	70,000,000
Add: NPV	1,151,000
New funds	2,835,000
New total MV	73,986,000
Existing number of shares	20,000,000
Add: New shares issued (2.835m/(3.50 × 0.9))	900,000
New number of shares	20,900,000
MV per share	3.54
Existing MV/cost	(3.15)
Gain per share	0.39

105 C

A is a result of assuming that a perfect capital market exists; it is not a conclusion

B is the Gordon growth model

D contradicts the dividend valuation model, which is not disputed by M&M

106 A

If a company announces that its long-term policy is to pay no dividends, the only investors in the shares should be investors seeking capital growth through reinvestment. Companies such as Microsoft have argued that shareholders needing cash can sell their shares in the market at any time, and so do not need dividends. The argument is also made that capital gains are not taxed until the shares are sold, which means that capital gains tax will be deferred, whereas tax on dividends would be an annual event. The tax treatment of capital gains is therefore favourable for investors seeking capital growth.

107 A, B, E

108 A, D

Debt may or may not be secured.

Interest returns are not guaranteed – for example if the company becomes bankrupt.

Transaction costs are assumed to be zero, a simplifying assumption of M&M's models.

109 A, D, E

Low returns on conserved cash will have a minimal impact on the share price.

There is no information given on other companies' performance.

The clientele A and signalling E effects both apply. Investors manufacturing dividends C will depress the share price.

110 Company X is planning on **decreasing** its dividend, but is concerned that the share price will fall.

This demonstrates the **signalling** effect.

111 A

The NPV of the project is equal to the increase in wealth of the shareholders (i.e. the increase in share price).

Therefore, an NPV of $6 million, split between 10 million shares means an increase of 6/10 = $0.60 per share.

112 A

Interest cover is (operating profit/interest payable)

= $305,000/[(10,000 × $100 × 4%) + ($500,000 × 2.5%)] = 5.8

113 B

Before the finance is raised:

Gearing = 100,000/(100,000 + (200,000 × $1.30)) = 27.8%

Interest cover = 25,000/(9% × 100,000) = 2.78

After the finance is raised:

Gearing = (100,000 + 40,000)/(100,000 + 40,000 + (200,000 × $1.25)) = 35.9%

Interest cover = 25,000/[(9% × 100,000) + (5% × 40,000)] = 2.27

114 B

The amount of cash required for the repurchase is 1 million shares at $0.40 each, so $0.40 million in total. Hence, cash will fall from $5 million to $4.6 million.

The new number of shares in issue will be (6 million − 1 million =) 5 million, so assuming that earnings stay constant, the EPS will be (total earnings/5 million).

Currently, earnings are $0.30 × 6 million = $1.80 million.

Therefore, EPS will be $1.80 million/5 million = $0.36 after the repurchase.

115 A, B

Debt

Interest = $60,000 and value of debt increases by $1m, so the ratios become:

Interest cover = (Earnings before interest and tax/Interest payable) = $1,600,000/$340,000 = 4.7 times

Earnings per share (EPS) = (Profit after tax/No. of shares) = $882,000/1,000,000 = $0.882

Note that profit after tax = (EBIT − Interest) × (1 − 0.30)

Gearing = (debt/equity) = $5m/$7m = 71.4%

Equity

250,000 extra shares and value of equity increases by $1m, so the ratios become:

Interest cover = (Earnings before interest and tax/Interest payable) = $1,600,000/$280,000 = 5.7 times

Earnings per share (EPS) = (Profit after tax/No. of shares) = $924,000/1,250,000 = $0.739

Gearing = (debt/equity) = $4m/$8m = 50.0%

116 C

Market value of debt is $50m × 0.99 = $49.5m

Current market value of equity is 40m × $3.14 = $125.6m, so after the share repurchase it will be $115.6m.

Therefore (D/(D+E)) = 49.5/(49.5 + 115.6) = 30.0%

117 C

Currently P/E is 8.55 and share price is $0.90.

Therefore, EPS = (0.90/8.55 =) $0.105

With 2 million shares in issue, this amounts to total earnings of approximately $210,000

After the issue, the project will add $50,000 earnings to this, so earnings will become $260,000.

Total shares will be 2 million existing shares + 1 million new ones (1 for 2 rights). Therefore 3 million in total.

Hence EPS will be 260,000/3 million = $0.087

118 C

Shareholder wealth is unaffected by a scrip dividend.

Consider a typical shareholder with 100 shares. Under the terms of the scrip dividend, this shareholder would receive an entitlement to one new share for every 10 held. That is, the right to acquire 10 new shares (where 10 = 100/10).

This may give the shareholder the illusion of increased 'value' as he now holds 110 shares. However, the company itself has not changed in value and so the total value that those shares represent is unchanged.

Therefore, the value of each share after the scrip issue will be ($1.65 × 100)/110 = $1.50

119 B

Debt will rise to $6.2m + $3m = $9.2m.

Equity will rise (because of the extra value generated by the takeover) to

$4m + $6.1m + $0.6m = $10.7m

Therefore, [D/(D+E)] = 9.2/(9.2 + 10.7) = 46.2%

120 A

Interest cover = 8.3m/(1m + (8% × 8m)) = 5.06 times

Capital gearing ratio

Debt = 10m + 8m +5m = $23m

Equity = 20m + 4m + 5m + 6m = $35m

D/(D+E) = 23m/(23m + 35m) × 100 = 39.7%

SYLLABUS SECTION C: CORPORATE FINANCE

121 A, D, E

The other points are reasons for a sell-off.

122 C

Asset stripping occurs when it is thought that the company is incorrectly valued and that the value of the assets is actually greater than the market capitalisation, and that the company could be purchased, broken up and the assets sold off for a profit.

123 A, B, D

After the management buyout, there are likely to be fewer economies of scale C as Spring Co is no longer part of a larger entity.

Although Spring Co no longer has to pay dividends to Season Co (E), it will now have to satisfy the bank and the venture capitalist, so there may be little difference in the overall amounts paid out.

124 D

The rate of return on equity is greater than that on debt, so venture capitalists like to provide finance in the form of equity. However, too much equity (more than the managers themselves have put in) would mean that the venture capitalists would control the business – a situation that would be unacceptable to the managers. Therefore, venture capitalists generally provide some equity finance to take a significant minority stake (e.g. 40% – 49%) and then provide the rest of the required funds in the form of debt finance.

125 B

The larger company uses its increased size and bargaining power to access cheaper debt finance.

126 A

Both companies operate in the same industry, even though they are in different countries. They are competitors and this is a horizontal acquisition.

127 B

128 C

Herra is purchasing a company that retails products that it manufactures. This is Vertical Integration.

129 C

The regulator is there to ensure that any proposed take-over is not anti-competitive and does not cause damage to the stakeholders.

130 D

The others are all post-bid defences.

131 B, D

A spin-off does not generate any cash A, or involve paying cash back to shareholders C. A MBO, not a spin-off, involves managers taking control (E).

132 C, D, E

A and B are post-bid defences.

133 B

Bootstrapping is a financial synergy.

134 B

135 C

Buying a controlling interest in a company, often from shareholders with little inclination to sell, requires a premium to be paid on acquisition (B and D). If there are likely to be synergies a premium can be paid without putting the wealth of the acquiring company's shareholders at risk.

136 B, C, D

A is false because this is horizontal, not vertical integration.

E is not a good reason for acquisition. Shareholders can diversify their own portfolios far more efficiently than companies can.

137 A

In a strongly efficient market, the prices would have moved BEFORE the information was made public. The markets here seem to be semi-strongly efficient.

138 A

Competition authorities can block a takeover B or allow it to proceed C. Sometimes conditions are imposed on the takeover, but these would apply to the public interest D rather than the value of the bid A which is perceived as being purely a matter for the two companies' shareholders.

139 D

The cost of capital is irrelevant when considering the likely profitability of a company.

140 B

The regulators will be interested in matters relating to the public interest and competition. They will have no interest in commercial factors, or what the directors of TT think of the takeover.

141 B

The DVM formula gives $0.60 \times 1.10/(0.13 - 0.10) = \$22.00$

But the quoted share price for a share that is just about to pay a dividend will be cum – dividend, i.e. $\$22.00 + \$0.60 = \$22.60$

142 E

Alpha is worth $3.2m, Beta is worth $16.8m, Gamma is worth $12m.

143 B

Expected value of FFF and GGG combined is:

9.5 × (5m + 3m + 0.5m) = $80.75 million

GGG's current value is

10 × 5m = $50 million.

Therefore the value of FFF to GGG is the difference between these two figures, i.e. $30.75 million.

144 B

CIMA's definition of free cash flow is 'Cash flow from operations after deducting interest, tax, preference dividends and ongoing capital expenditure, but excluding capital expenditure associated with strategic acquisitions and/or disposals and ordinary share dividends.'

	$000
Operating profit	879
Interest	(210)
Taxable profit	669
Tax at 22%	(147)
Profit after tax	522
Add: Depreciation	167
Investment in NCA	(378)
Investment in WC	(143)
FREE CASH FLOW	168

145 D

One way of valuing the equity of a firm is to forecast the free cash flows and then discount at the cost of equity.

CIMA's definition of free cash flow is 'Cash flow from operations after deducting interest, tax, preference dividends and ongoing capital expenditure, but excluding capital expenditure associated with strategic acquisitions and/or disposals and ordinary share dividends.'

Thus A is not correct as dividends should not be deducted and C is not correct as taxation should be deducted (and also the cost of equity should be used as the discount rate, not WACC).

An alternative way of valuing the equity is to value the whole entity (debt + equity) and then subtract the market value of debt to be left with the market value of equity. With this method we would discount post-tax cash flows BEFORE financing charges using the WACC to get the value of the entity. Then we would deduct the MV of the debt to get the MV of the equity.

B is nearly correct then, but it should be post-tax cash flows BEFORE financing charges being discounted not free cash flows.

146   B

Forecast post-tax cash flows before financing charges should be discounted at WACC to give the value of the entity, and then the value of debt should be deducted to give the value of equity.

	T1	T2	T3	T4
$m	283	291	298	305
12%	0.893	0.797	0.712	0.636
PV	253	232	212	194

Value of the perpetuity from T5 to perpetuity is:

$[(305 \times 1.03)/(0.12-0.03)] \times 0.636 = 2,220$

Value of the entity = $3,111m (The sum of the PVs)

And therefore the value of the equity (70%) is $2,178m

147   A

$\$23.12m(1.05)/(0.12 - 0.05) = \$346.80m$

148   C

$\$1.5m(1.04)/(0.14 - 0.04) = \$15.6$ million. There are 1 million shares, so $15.60 per share.

149   C

A high P/E ratio often indicates that a high rate of growth of earnings is expected from a company.

150   C

P/E ratio = Share price/Earnings per share

Earnings per share is calculated as profit after tax after the deduction of preference share dividends = $17,000 − $2,000 = $15,000/70,000 = 21.4c per share.

= 204/21.4

= 9.5

151   B

Answer A is possible but only for companies with a temporary dip in profits. Answer C is also possible but the EMH implies that all shares are correctly priced and so a share cannot be 'overpriced'.

152   D

The dividend yield is 2% and the dividend cover is 4.

Dividend yield = Dividend/Share price

Dividend cover = Earnings/Dividends

Therefore earnings as a percentage of share price = dividend yield × dividend cover

Therefore earnings are (2% × 4) = 8% of the price.

The price must be 100/8 × 20 cents = 250 cents

153   B

The dividend per share is 2c

As the dividend cover is 4, the earnings per share are 8c

The price per share is thus 10 × 8c = 80c

There are $2 million of 25c shares = 8 million shares so the market value is 8 million × 80c = $6.4 million

154   C

$500,000/$0.25 × $2.30 = $4,600,000

155   D

As the company intends to list on the market, the shareholders are entitled to receive future dividends and hence the dividend valuation model is the correct method to use in this case.

156   The answer is **$0.102m**

((4.10 + 1.30) × 42%) + 0.32 + (0.45 × 72%) less (0.66 + 2.15) = $0.102m

157 The answer is

EPS	$3.71
Value per share using dividend valuation model	$36.23
Value per share using the P/E model	$42.67

Workings:

EPS = $11.12m/3m = $3.71

Dividend Valuation Model:

g = rb

r = ke = 11% or 0.11

b = (11.12–3.34)/11.12 = 0.70

g= 0.11 × 0.70 = 0.077

Dividend per share = $3.34m/3m = $1.11

Po = $1.11(1.077) /(0.11–0.077) = **$36.23**

P/E Valuation

P/E ratio of Zudun Co is $598m/$52m = 11.5

Po = $3.71 × 11.5 = **$42.67**

158 B

Total value is $259,000 × 14 = $3,626,000

Value per share is $3,626,000/1m = $3.63

159 C

Dividend cover = earnings/dividends

So Earnings = dividends × dividend cover

Abbott Co earnings = $2m × 5 = $10m

Total value = 10 × $10m = $100m

160 A

The sale of land cannot happen again and the profit after tax used in the valuation must be sustainable for the future. Therefore we need to first remove the land profit from the profit after tax.

Sustainable profit after tax = 1.5 – 0.325 = $1.175 million

Total value of equity = 8 × $1.175 million = $9.4 million

161 B

The total value is $800,000 × 10 = $8 million, but this needs to be reduced for non-marketability as an unlisted company is not worth as much as a listed company.

In this case we need to reduce by 25%

Value of Veena Co = $8 million × 75% = $6 million

162 B

The current profit after tax needs to be adjusted for the directors' salaries to give a sustainable earnings figure for the valuation.

The after tax cost of the salaries is $40,000 × (1 – 0.30) = $28,000

So the adjusted earnings is $500,000 – $28,000 = $472,000

Total value is $472,000 × 5 = $2,360,000

163 C

Strong form market efficiency assumes that all information, both public and private, is reflected in a company's share price.

As the expansion strategy had been planned internally for a period of months, this private information would be included in the share price.

164 C

The preferred approach is a good spread of shares, as this minimises the risk in the portfolio and should ensure that Miss Coates does achieve something approaching the average return for the market.

165 B

166 The answer is

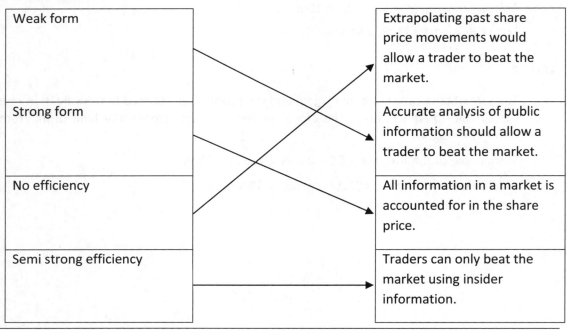

Weak form	Extrapolating past share price movements would allow a trader to beat the market.
Strong form	Accurate analysis of public information should allow a trader to beat the market.
No efficiency	All information in a market is accounted for in the share price.
Semi strong efficiency	Traders can only beat the market using insider information.

167 D

(1) The expected NPV of a project has nothing to do with the efficiency of the market. Even though, with strong-form efficiency, a project's positive NPV is incorporated within the share price as soon as the project is devised and accepted, this does not deny the fact that the project has a positive NPV. Hence the existence of projects with a positive expected NPV neither supports nor contradicts the idea that the market is strong-form efficient. Therefore, false.

(2) Strong-form efficiency states that the share price already includes all relevant information when a dividend is declared and the dividend adds no information. Therefore, false.

168 A

Current pre-tax profit generated from the intangibles is $453 - (1268 \times 15\%) = 262.8$ ($000)

Assuming this value is a pre-tax cash flow occurring from T1 until perpetuity and discounted at the company WACC is $(262.8(1-0.30))/0.11 = \$1.672m$

169 A

First of all we need to find a suitable ungeared beta

De-gear

$\beta_u = \beta_g \times E/(E + D(1-t))$

$\beta_u = 1.8 \times 50/(50 + 50(1 - 0.30))$

$\beta_u = 1.06$

Then use this to find an appropriate βg

$\beta_u = \beta_g \times E/(E + D(1-t))$

$1.06 = \beta_g \times 60/(60 + 40(1 - 0.30))$

$1.06 = \beta_g \times 0.682$

$B_g = 1.06/0.682 = 1.55$

Use CAPM

$K_{eg} = R_f + \beta(R_m - Rf)$

$K_{eg} = 0.05 + 1.55 (0.08 - 0.05) = 9.65\%$

170 B

$(0.333)(0.06) + (0.333)(0.10) + 0.333(.05) = 0.07$

171 A

De-gear

$\beta_u = \beta_g \times E/(E + D(1-t))$

$\beta_u = 0.9 \times 2/(2+0.7)$

$\beta_u = 0.6667$

Use CAPM

$K_{eg} = R_f + \beta(R_m - R_f)$

$K_{eg} = 2 + 0.6667 \times (8-2)$

$K_{eg} = 6.00\%$

172 D

Re-gear

$\beta_u = \beta_g \times E/(E + D(1-t))$

$0.9 = \beta_g \times 2/(2.7)$

$B_g = 1.215$

Use CAPM

$K_{eg} = R_f + \beta(R_m - R_f)$

$K_{eg} = 2 + 1.215 \times 8$

$K_{eg} = 11.72\%$

173 B

Use CAPM

$K_{eg} = R_f + \beta(R_m - R_f)$

$K_{eg} = 2\% + 0.9 \times 8\%$

$K_{eg} = 9.20\%$

174 C

Re-gear

$\beta_u = \beta_g \times E/(E + D(1-t))$

$0.9 = \beta_g \times 2/(2.7)$

$B_g = 1.215$

Use CAPM

$K_{eg} = R_f + \beta(R_m - R_f)$

$K_{eg} = 2 + 1.215 \times (8-2)$

$K_{eg} = 9.29\%$

175 A

Use CAPM

$K_{eg} = R_f + \beta(R_m - R_f)$

$K_{eg} = 2\% + 0.9 \times (8\% - 2\%)$

$K_{eg} = 7.40\%$

176 C

$$\beta_g = \beta_u + \left[(\beta_u - \beta_d)\left(\frac{Ve(1-t)}{Vd}\right) \right]$$

where Ve and Vd are the equity and debt values for our company (SIX Co in this case), and βu is the ungeared equity beta of APPLE Co, calculated as:

$$\beta_u = \left[1.45 \times \frac{70}{70 + 30(1 - 0.25)} \right] + \left[0.10 \times \frac{30(1 - 0.25)}{70 + 30(1 - 0.25)} \right] = 1.12$$

The correct answer is the third on the list.

177 B

If all the companies are facing the same business risk then their asset betas will be the same. The only difference for the equity beta will be the level of financial risk that they cause their shareholders. The gearing of Tarte Co is higher than company B's, but lower than company A's and so Tarte Co's equity beta will be between the two.

178 A

First of all we need to find a suitable ungeared beta

De-gear

$\beta_u = \beta_g \times E/(E + D(1-t))$

$\beta_u = 1.2 \times 70/(70 + 30(1 - 0.30)$

$\beta_u = 0.92$

Then use this to find an appropriate βg

$\beta_u = \beta_g \times E/(E + D(1-t))$

$0.92 = \beta_g \times 85/(85 + 15(1 - 0.30))$

$0.92 = \beta_g \times 0.890$

$B_g = 0.92/0.890 = 1.034$

Use CAPM

$K_{eg} = R_f + \beta(R_m - R_f)$

$K_{eg} = 0.04 + 1.034(0.10 - 0.04) = 10.2\%$

Therefore WACC = $(10.2\% \times 85/100) + (4\% \times (1-0.30) \times 15/100) = 9.1\%$

179 B

First of all we need to de-gear the current equity beta

De-gear

$\beta_u = \beta_g \times E/(E + D(1\text{-}t))$

$\beta_u = 1.4 \times 70/(70 + 30(1 - 0.3))$

$\beta_u = 1.08$

This will then be used in the cost of equity

$K_{eu} = R_f + \beta_u(R_m - R_f)$

$K_{eu} = 0.05 + 1.08 \times 0.07$

$K_{eu} = 12.6\%$

180 C

First of all we need to find a suitable ungeared beta

De-gear

$\beta_u = \beta_g \times E/(E + D(1\text{-}t))$

$\beta_u = 1.6 \times 80/(80 + 20(1 - 0.3)$

$\beta_u = 1.36$

Then use this to find an appropriate βg

$\beta_u = \beta_g \times E/(E + D(1\text{-}t))$

$1.36 = \beta_g \times 70/(70 + 30(1 - 0.30))$

$1.36 = \beta_g \times 0.769$

$B_g = 1.36/ 0.769 = 1.77$

Use CAPM

$K_{eg} = R_f + \beta(R_m - Rf)$

$K_{eg} = 0.04 + 1.77(0.08 - 0.04) = 11.1\%$

181 A

The VC is making a $15 million equity investment. To generate a return of 20% a year on a compound basis this investment will need to grow to $25.92 million (=$15 million × (1.20)3) at the end of 3 years.

The VC investment represents 37.5% (= 15/(15+25) × 100%) of the equity, therefore the total equity value will need to be $69.12 million (= $25.92 million/0.375).

182 C, D, E

183 B

A cash offer funded by debt would increase A's gearing C and would prevent the B shareholders from participating in the future growth of the company D.

Since no A shares are being issued, the control of A's shareholders would stay the same A.

184 D

Value of merged company ($ million) = 30 + 10 + 6 + 2 = $48 million

Spain Co's shareholders have 75%, so France Co's shareholders have 25% (i.e. $12 million)

This is a gain of $2 million.

185 B

If GGG Co buys another company and values the target company on a higher P/E ratio, and if there is no synergy, there will be a reduction in the earnings per share of GGG Co D. Since the acquisition is paid for by using new shares, the gearing ratio of GGG Co will fall A, and existing shareholders will own a smaller proportionate stake in the company C. It is unlikely that the share price will increase; in view of the reduction in earnings per share, it is more likely that the share price will fall after the takeover.

186 B, D

Stone Co has high gearing so increasing gearing further would be unwise ((A) and (E)).

Low cash reserves would rule out a cash offer funded from existing resources C.

With a wide range of shareholders, a rights issue should be successful D, or a share for share exchange could be used B because none of the existing shareholders seem to have control, so they would be less concerned about dilution issues.

187 A

Total value of the combined company will be:

(12m × $6.76) + (3m × $1.97) + 2m = $89.03m

The number of shares in the combined company will be:

12 m + [(1/3) × 3m] = 13m

Therefore the share price will be $89.03m/13m = $6.85

188 C

Bootstrapping can be used to find the post-acquisition value of combined companies assuming that the buying company's P/E ratio exceeds that of the seller.

The value is computed by applying Udika's P/E ratio to the combined current earnings of both entities.

189 A

190 A

Current values:

Oban 126m shares × $4.00 = $504m

Reeves 20m × $4.25 = $85m

Total is $589m

Oban's EPS = $25.2m/126m shares = $0.20

Oban's P/E ratio = $4.00/$0.20 = 20

Post-acquisition values

Oban's PAT = $25.2m

Reeves PAT = 20m shares × $0.34 = $6.8m

Combined PAT = $32m

Value using Oban's P/E = $32m × 20 = $640m

Synergy valued at $640 – $589 = $51m

191 C

A, B and D certainly would be problems in this situation.

The fact that Fitness Co has very little cash C is irrelevant. In a share for share exchange no cash is paid.

192 A

Current wealth is $6.90 × 30 million = $207 million

After the takeover, total value of the combined entity will be

$207 million + $8 million + (5m × $12.84) = $279.2 million

There will be 40 million shares in issue (being 30 million existing shares and 10 million new shares issued in the share exchange with JJJ).

Hence, MMM's shareholders will own 30/40 = 75% of the combined entity, with a value of (75% × $279.2 million =) $209.4 million.

So the gain in wealth is $2.4 million ($209.4 million – $207 million).

193 The market believes that the shareholders of **YZ** will receive most of the benefit from this acquisition.

This could be because the value of the offer is too **high**.

194 Compared to a cash offer, a share for share exchange is **less** likely to create a liability to capital gains tax.

A share for share exchange will benefit the target company's shareholders more than a cash offer if the combined entity performs **well** after the acquisition.

195 C

An earnout would make some of the consideration dependent of future performance, so the directors of Z would be encouraged to continue working for the combined company and to improve its performance as much as possible.

196 D

Given the current share prices, it appears that the MQ shareholders would be indifferent if an offer of 2.23 LP shares to 1 MQ share were offered. However, they would be more likely to accept a bid that offered them a premium over the current value, so the best of the four choices – D in this case – is the MOST likely to be acceptable.

197 B

Current value of Astor Co = (23.5 × 9 =) $211.5 million

Current value of Baker Co = (9.5 × 7 =) $66.5 million

So the total value of the two companies is $278.0 million

Bootstrapping means applying the larger company's P/E ratio to the combined earnings, so post acquisition value = 9 × (23.5 + 9.5) = $297.0 million

i.e. a gain of $19.0 million

198 B

Value of Glenderaterra Co = $3.88 × 50m = $194.0 million

Value of Mungrisdale Co = $1.10 × 12m = $13.2 million

Therefore, value of the combined entity will be $194.0m + $13.2m + $10m = $217.2 million

Number of shares in the combined entity will be 50m + [(1/3) × 12m] = 54 million

Hence the share price post acquisition will be ($217.2m/54m) = $4.02

Mungrisdale Co shareholders will hold 4 million of the combined entity's shares, with a total value of $16.08 million. This is a gain of (16.08 – 13.2 =) $2.88 million.

i.e. approximately 29% of the total gain of $10 million

199 C

A debt for share exchange enables the target company shareholders to maintain an interest in the combined entity, but preserves the balance of control for the bidding company's shareholders C.

If the target company shareholders want to realise cash for their investment A or if the bidding company is highly geared B, a debt for share exchange would not be suitable.

D is irrelevant.

200 C

Current wealth is $6.90 × 30 million = $207 million

After the takeover, total value of the combined entity will be

$207 million + $8 million + (5m × $12.84) = $279.2 million

Since JJJ's shareholders' share of this value is the cash received of ($13.50 × 5 million =) $67.5 million, MMM's share will be (balancing figure) $211.7 million, which is $4.7 million more than it was before.